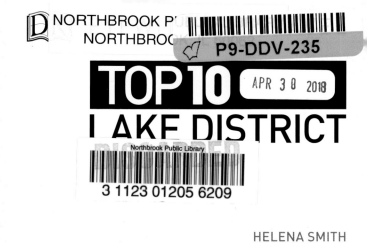

TOP 10

LAKE DISTRICT

HELENA SMITH

Penguin
Random
House

Top 10 Lake District Highlights

The Top 10 of Everything

CONTENTS

Lake District Area by Area

Streetsmart

Within each Top 10 list in this book, no hierarchy of quality or popularity is implied. All 10 are, in the editor's opinion, of roughly equal merit.

Front cover and spine *Mountains reflected in idyllic Wast Water, Wasdale*
Back cover *Traditional row boats on the shore of Derwent Water, near Keswick*
Title page *Kirk Fell and Great Gable as seen from Illgill Head, Wasdale*

Welcome to
The Lake District

Rich autumnal colours reflected in mirror-clear lake water. Boulder-strewn mountains – known here as fells – and soft green valleys grazed by sheep. Tiny villages of whitewashed stone. Bustling markets, cosy country inns and Michelin-starred restaurants. This region is all this and more. With Eyewitness Top 10 Lake District, it's yours to explore.

Rising up above England's windswept northwestern coastline, the Lake District's wild peaks, rolling farmland, placid waters and winding country lanes have sunk themselves deep into the national psyche. As the inspiration behind William Wordsworth's and Samuel Taylor Coleridge's Romantic poetry, Arthur Ransome's children's adventures and, of course, Beatrix Potter's tales, this landscape has deeply influenced the way in which we picture the British countryside.

Central to the region, pretty **Grasmere** village was once home to Wordsworth himself. Nearby **Windermere**, England's largest lake, offers boat rides, easy walks and attractive **Ambleside** town, while **Coniston Water** also boasts a Victorian steamboat. **Kendal**, the Lakes' southern gateway, hosts good wet-weather attractions, as does its northern counterpart **Keswick**. For off-the-beaten-track appeal, it's hard to beat **Langdale** or **Wasdale**, two isolated valleys where facilities are few but the scenery is tremendous.

Whether you're visiting for a weekend or a week, our Top 10 guide brings together the best of everything the Lake District has to offer, from walking in the footsteps of Alfred Wainwright to gazing on Wordsworth's beloved golden daffodils. The guide gives you tips throughout, from seeking out what's free to avoiding the crowds, plus seven easy-to-follow itineraries, designed to help you visit a clutch of sights in a short space of time. Add inspiring photography and detailed maps, and you've got the essential pocket-sized travel companion. **Enjoy the book, and enjoy the Lake District.**

Clockwise from top: **Old Man of Coniston; Cat Bells seen from Ashness Bridge; Castle Crag;** valley south of Keswick; Lake District cattle; summit of Skiddaw; boats on Windermere

Exploring the Lake District

The Lake District packs a huge amount into a very small area – while you can spend a whole day cruising around a lake, hiking a hillside or exploring a town, it doesn't take long to drive between sights, and many are accessible by public transport, too. Here are two itineraries to help you make the most of your visit.

Cockermouth

Honister Pass

Wasdale

Eskdale

Ravenglass and Eskdale Railway

Muncaster Castle

Wasdale represents the Lake District at its wildest.

Two Days in the Lake District

Day ❶

MORNING

Kick off your tour on **Windermere**'s eastern shore (see pp14–15) at the fine Arts and Crafts manor house of **Blackwell** (see p15), then take a cruise (see p15) along the lake itself.

AFTERNOON

Cross the lake to **Hill Top** (see p15), Beatrix Potter's farm. Afterwards, head on to the charming village of **Hawkshead** (see p71) and end the day at **Coniston** (see p30), both rich in pubs and literary associations.

Day ❷

MORNING

Start the day at the **Ruskin Museum** in **Coniston** (see p31), then cruise the lake aboard the **Gondola** steamboat (see p30) – or even make a stiff ascent of the **Old Man of Coniston** (see p30) for breathtaking views.

AFTERNOON

Drive up dramatic **Langdale** (see pp24–5), taking in views of the

Crinkle Crags (see p24), **Chapel Stile** village (see p25) and **Colwith Force** waterfall (see p25). Then aim for Wordsworth's home village of **Grasmere** (see p12–13), dotted with sites from the poet's life, including **Dove Cottage** (see p79).

Seven Days in the Lake District

Days ❶ and ❷

Follow the two-day Lake District itinerary as the perfect introduction.

Blackwell is a magnificently preserved Arts and Crafts manor house.

Key
— Two-day itinerary
▬▬ Seven-day itinerary

Helvellyn, England's third-highest summit, is challenging to climb all year round.

Day ❺

Head down the coast to **Muncaster Castle** (see p74), said to be Britain's most haunted castle, then backtrack inland to **Wasdale** (see p32–3), overlooked by a host of dramatic crags, including **Scafell Pike** (see p33), England's highest peak.

Day ❻

Pass through attractive Eskdale – enthusiasts will want to ride the little **Ravenglass and Eskdale Railway** (see p53) here – before tackling the challenging drive east over **Hardknott Pass** (see p52), with its ruined Roman fort. Stay in little **Ambleside** town (see p20–21).

Day ❼

Visit tiny **Cartmel** (see p74), famed for its priory and its Michelin-starred restaurant, before having brunch at **Grange-over-Sands** (see p74). Spend the afternoon at child-friendly **Low Sizergh Barn** or **Sizergh Castle** (see p16), before leaving the Lake District via **Kendal** (see pp16–17).

Kendal is a typical and charming Lake District market town.

Day ❸

Head up between **Thirlmere** and **Helvellyn** (see p90) to **Keswick** (see p34–5). Drop in to the **Derwent Pencil Museum** (see p35), and then make a circuit eastwards to **Aira Force** (see p91) and **Pooley Bridge** (see p89), before returning to Keswick for the evening.

Day ❹

Catch the sunrise at **Castlerigg Stone Circle** (see p35) and then loop south through **Borrowdale** (see pp18–19), possibly detouring to stretch your legs and take in views of **Derwent Water** (see p18) from atop **Cat Bells** (see p97). Cross windswept **Honister Pass** (see p96) and descend to the pleasant Georgian town of **Cockermouth** (see p95).

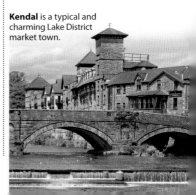

0 km — 8
0 miles — 8

Top 10 Lake District Highlights

Skiddaw mountain, near Keswick

TOP10 Lake District Highlights

The Lake District, a UNESCO World Heritage site, is one of the most beautiful, romantic parts of Britain, with spectacular peaks, verdant valleys and, of course, plenty of lakes. It is a great place for outdoor activities – each evening every pub plays host to weary hikers. The Lakes were put on the tourist map by William Wordsworth, and local residents have long provided visitors with hearty food, good ale and a soft bed. Wild it may be, but domestic comforts are never far away.

1 Grasmere
This pretty village is encircled by high fells and isolated tarns, and replete with teashops and stone cottages. Wordsworth's famous Dove Cottage is close at hand (see pp12–13).

2 Windermere
It's a must to take a cruise on England's largest lake. The surrounding area is rich in fine historic homes (see pp14–15).

3 Kendal
A gateway town to the South Lakes, Kendal is a hub of arty activity and home to some good restaurants (see pp16–17).

Borrowdale 4
Thickly wooded Borrowdale is scattered with stone farmhouses and villages, many in the shadow of high fells (see pp18–19).

5 Ambleside
Centrally located, this bustling little town makes an excellent base for a holiday in the Lakes (see pp20–21).

6 Langdale
With high peaks, tumbling waterfalls, country pubs and hiking opportunities galore, Langdale should not be missed *(see pp24–5)*.

7 Wordsworth's Lake District
The region is scattered with sights associated with Wordsworth and his sister Dorothy, whose notebooks inspired some of his best poems *(see pp26–9)*.

8 Coniston Water
This lake was Arthur Ransome's inspiration for his much-loved *Swallows and Amazons* children's books; as a child, he spent his holidays at Nibthwaite, at Coniston's southern end *(see pp30–31)*.

9 Wasdale
One of the most remote and scenic parts of the area, where you can go for hikes, pitch a tent or stay at Wasdale Head Inn *(see pp32–3)*.

Keswick 10
It may be a workaday town in the northern Lake District, but it is one with terrific museums, markets, theatres and amenities. Keswick also has iconic walks, as well as Derwent Water, nearby *(see pp34–5)*.

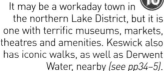

TOP 10 ⭐ Grasmere

Sitting in the middle of the Central Fells, Grasmere, with handsome stone cottages and lush surroundings, is the archetypal Lake District settlement. Home to Wordsworth and his extended family for 12 years, the village features all the pleasures of the region rolled into one. There are rugged walks to isolated tarns and peaks, watersports on Grasmere lake, an early medieval church and a range of independent shops and galleries. And of course, this being the Lakes, a cream tea or a pint is always close by.

1 Hike to Easedale Tarn

A signed path **(above)** leads northwest from the village for the three-hour round trip to Easedale Tarn, a lake ringed by magnificent peaks. A steep but satisfying hike.

2 Coffin Trail

The name refers to the fact that this route, which runs from Grasmere to Rydal then Ambleside, was used by coffin bearers taking bodies for burial at St Oswald's. It is a lovely, stretching walk.

3 Dove Cottage

Wordsworth lived here from 1799 to 1808 with sister Dorothy, wife Mary and their family. There are guided tours of the cottage **(right)** and exhibitions at the museum next door.

4 Rowing on the Lake

Rent a boat **(above)** at the Faeryland Tea Garden just south of the village to experience some wonderful views of the surrounding fells. Then return to Faeryland for a pot of tea and cake.

5 Wordsworth Museum

This is one of the best museums in the Lakes, featuring portraits of Wordsworth and his contemporaries, letters, journals, poems and plenty of fascinating memorabilia.

7 St Oswald's Church

At the heart of Grasmere is the bulky church of St Oswald **(left)**, which has a 13th-century nave and a timber roof. The Wordsworths are buried in the graveyard.

Grasmere

DE QUINCEY IN GRASMERE

Thomas de Quincey, author of *Confessions of an English Opium Eater* (1821), came to stay with the Wordsworths in Grasmere in 1807. He had been addicted to opium since the age of 19, having first taken it in the form of laudanum for neuralgia. When the Wordsworths moved to Allan Bank, de Quincey took over Dove Cottage, and his relationship with the poet, whom he had admired to the point of adulation, began to cool.

8 Sarah Nelson's Gingerbread Shop

The warm, spicy smell of gingerbread – made to a secret recipe since the mid-19th century – will lead you to this shop next to the churchyard. Housed in a quaint cottage, it is staffed by ladies in mob caps *(see p62)*.

10 Sam Read's Bookshop

This great little shop **(above)** has a wide range of local publications, including a strong fiction section and lots of books for kids. The owner is likely to have read any title you ask about.

6 Greenhead Ghyll

Just east of the village, a path runs along the Ghyll, which features in Wordsworth's *Michael* as "the tumultuous brook".

9 Heaton Cooper Studio

This gallery has been run by the same family since 1905 and features works by Alfred and William Heaton Cooper, as well as prints and sculptures.

NEED TO KNOW

MAP E5

Dove Cottage and Wordsworth Museum: SE of Grasmere; 015394 35544; 9:30am–5pm daily (4pm in winter), closed Jan; adm £8.95 (covers both sites); www.wordsworth.org.uk

Sarah Nelson's Gingerbread Shop: Church Cottage; 015394 35428; 9:15am–5pm Mon–Sat, 12:30–5pm Sun (closing times vary in winter; call for details); www.grasmeregingerbread.co.uk

Heaton Cooper Studio: The Green; 015394 35280; 9am–5:30pm Mon–Sat (5pm in winter), 10am–5pm Sun; www.heatoncooper.co.uk

Sam Read's Bookshop: Broadgate House; 015394 35374; 9am–6pm daily (5pm in winter)

■ Jumble Room on Langdale Road is a good choice for dinner *(see p85)*.

TOP 10 ⭐ Windermere

The lakeside town of Windermere is a transport hub for the region due to its train station; Windermere also has the railway to thank for the grey stone guesthouses and impressive villas that were built in the Victorian period. The town does not have the intimate feel of other Lake District settlements, but there are some superb hotels nearby, and the lake – England's largest – is wonderful to explore by cruise, canoe or rowing boat. Some unique sights are dotted around the lake, chief among them Townend and Blackwell.

View at sunrise over Windermere

1 Wray Castle
This lavish folly **(below)** was built as a holiday home in the 19th century. It's perfect for a family day out, with house tours and gardens overlooking Windermere.

2 Townend
One of the area's most compelling sights is 17th-century Townend. This rugged stone and slate building, with round chimneys and a wood-clad interior, was owned by a family of local farmers for centuries.

3 Windermere Jetty: Museum of Boats, Steam and Stories
In a stunning lakeside location, this museum has a splendid collection of historic vessels and steam launches.

4 Fell Foot
This park, run by the National Trust, is a great location for picnics, watersports and other outdoor activities. There are swathes of daffodils in early spring.

5 Lakeside & Haverthwaite Railway
The gleaming, quaint steam engines of the Lakeside & Haverthwaite Railway chug all the way through the Leven Valley, making a scenic journey from Haverthwaite Station to Lakeside.

6 Blackwell

Set high above Windermere with its stunning views over the lake, this Arts and Crafts House is a masterpiece of 20th-century design. It was designed by M H Baillie-Scott as a holiday home for Sir Edward Holt. It still has all of its original features, including the wood-panelled great hall.

7 Stott Park Bobbin Mill

The 19th-century bobbin mill **(below)** provides an insight into the grim industrial past. There are guided tours for visitors.

9 Hill Top

This 17th-century farmhouse is a must-see for Beatrix Potter fans. It is furnished with many of the author's possessions and the museum has plenty of Potter memorabilia on display. "Mr McGregor's Garden" includes some familiar little rabbits for children to spot.

10 Walk to Orrest Head

From the northern end of the town, the steep walk up to Orrest Head runs high above the lake and offers great views.

THE CULT OF BEATRIX POTTER

A perennially popular attraction can be found in the town of Bowness-on-Windermere: The World of Beatrix Potter. With its interactive activities and shopping opportunities, it is fair to say that this commercial endeavour might not have been approved by the author. Fans should visit Hill Top instead, or explore the fells on foot with one of her charming books as a companion.

Windermere

8 Lake Cruises

A cruise on Windermere **(below)** is not to be missed. Admire the scenery, hop around nearby islands and explore the Lakeland villages.

NEED TO KNOW

Wray Castle: **MAP F6**; Low Wray; 015394 33250; castle: 10am–4pm Sat–Sun; grounds: 8am–8pm daily; adm £9 (adult), £4.50 (child), £22.50 (family)

Townend: **MAP N1**; S of Troutbeck; 015394 32628; mid-Mar–Oct: 1–5pm Wed–Sun; adm £5.90

Windermere Jetty: Museum of Boats, Steam and Stories: **MAP N2**; Rayrigg Rd; 015394 46139; closed until 2018

Fell Foot: **MAP N3**; Newby Bridge; 015395 31273; 9am–5pm

Lakeside & Haverthwaite Railway: **MAP M3**; S Windermere; 015395 31594; £6.80 adult return

Blackwell: **MAP N2**; Bowness-on-Windermere; 015394 46139; 10.30am–5pm daily; adm £8

Stott Park Bobbin Mill: **MAP N3**; Ulverston; 015395 31087; Apr–Oct: 11am–5pm Mon–Fri (Jul–Aug: daily); adm £7.60

Lake Cruises: 015394 43360; £8.25–20

Hill Top: **MAP M2**; Near Sawrey; 015394 36269; mid-Mar–Oct: 10:30am–3:30pm Sat–Thu (Easter–May: to 4:30pm, Jun–Aug: 10am–5:30pm); adm £10.40

TOP 10 ⭐ Kendal

Although Kendal sits outside the boundaries of the Lake District National Park, it is the introduction to the region for many visitors, as it is on the train line from Oxenholme. The handsome little market town has many of the most appealing characteristics of the Lakes: fine stone buildings, independent shops and restaurants, and verdant hills surrounding it. The two unmissable attractions here are the Abbot Hall Art Gallery and the Museum of Lakeland Life and Industry.

1 Brewery Arts Centre

This cosmopolitan arts venue (above) has two cinema screens, a theatre, an exhibition space, a bar, a café and a restaurant. Workshops and courses are also offered. It is housed in a dramatic terraced stone building that was once a brewery.

2 Walk to the Castle Ruins

The circular stone walls and tall towers of the 12th-century Kendal Castle are visible wherever you are in town. The steep walk to the castle provides a pretty view of the town and surrounding countryside.

3 Lakeland Climbing Centre

Great on a rainy day, the climbing walls offer 250 different routes, so there's something for everyone, from serious mountaineers to kids.

4 Low Sizergh Barn

A working dairy farm, Low Sizergh has a free farm trail. The 17th-century timbered barn has an award-winning farm shop (below) and a fine café.

5 Sizergh Castle

This impressive castle was extended in the 16th century; highlights include oak interiors and a limestone rock garden. It has been home to the same family for almost 800 years.

Museum of Lakeland Life and Industry ⑥

Engaging, educational and beautiful displays **(right)** create a step-back-in-time feel. Browse in Edwardian shops, peek into a lead mine and walk into the parlour of a Lakeland farm.

KENDAL MINT CAKE

Kendal is the home of the astonishingly sweet confection Kendal Mint Cake, first made here in 1869. The dense, sugary mint sometimes comes wrapped in chocolate. It is famous both for its tooth-rotting qualities, and for giving a boost to flagging fell-walkers. According to legend, it was invented as a result of a culinary accident.

⑧ Abbot Hall Art Gallery

A range of contemporary, high-profile art shows are held in this listed villa set beside the river Kent. The gallery also features a fine collection of works by local artist George Romney.

⑩ Quaker Tapestry

This tapestry, in Kendal Meeting house, consists of 77 embroidered panels and interactive displays, revealing a wealth of social history.

⑨ Levens Hall

An imposing Elizabethan home, Levens Hall is decked with rich furnishings, oak panelling and leather wall-coverings, as well as what is thought to be the oldest topiary garden in the world **(below)**.

⑦ Kendal Museum

Alfred Wainwright *(see p54)* once worked here. The collection includes local Roman and Viking finds and there are also displays on wildlife and natural history.

NEED TO KNOW

Brewery Arts Centre:
MAP S3; Highgate; 01539 725133; noon–10:30pm Mon, 10am–10:30pm Tue–Sat, 2–8:30pm Sun

Lakeland Climbing Centre: **MAP P2**; Lake District Business Park; 01539 721766; 9am–5:30pm Mon–Sat, 10am–5:30pm Sun

Low Sizergh Barn:
MAP P3; 015395 60426; 9am–5:30pm daily

Sizergh Castle: **MAP P3**; 015395 60951; castle: Apr–Oct: noon–4pm Tue–Sun; gardens: 10am–5pm daily, closed Jan; adm £10.50

Museum of Lakeland Life and Industry: 10:30am–5pm Mon–Sat, adm £5

Kendal Museum: **MAP T1**; Station Road; 01539

721374; 10:30am–5pm Tue–Sat

Abbot Hall Art Gallery:
MAP T3; 01539 722464; adm £7

Levens Hall: **MAP P3**; 015395 60321; Easter–Oct: noon–5pm Sun–Thu; adm £12.50

Quaker Tapestry: **MAP T2**; Stramongate; 01539 722975; mid-Feb–mid-Dec: 10am–5pm Mon–Sat; adm £7

TOP10 ⭐ Borrowdale

Lush and heavily wooded, the valley of Borrowdale has a distinctly otherwordly air, as befits its name, which could be straight out of a Tolkien novel. The trees seem to be taller here than elsewhere, the crags higher, the fells soar far above, and the valley bottom is dense with enormous ferns, yews and oaks. There are some lovely little villages clustered along the river Derwent, and you will find plenty of opportunities for fell walks, as well as a range of watersports on nearby Derwent Water.

3 Rosthwaite
The whitewashed cottages **(left)** of tiny Rosthwaite provide some of the most attractive accommodation in the region. If you are here on the first Saturday of August you will be in prime position for the Borrowdale Fell Race.

NEED TO KNOW
MAP D4

■ The regularity of the Borrowdale Rambler (Apr–Oct) makes public transport a very good option in this beautiful part of the Lake District.

■ There is nowhere prettier for tea and cakes than the riverside Grange Bridge Cottage Teashop *(see p101)*.

1 Castle Crag
This is a lovely walk that runs from Grange up a peak that peers over the treetops and provides great views of Borrowdale. Castle Crag may have been the site of an ancient fort, which explains the name.

4 The Bowder Stone
This giant stone is a rather peculiar but mesmerizing attraction, thought to have been transported here from Scotland via a glacier. You can ascend it by a wooden ladder.

2 Derwent Water
A footpath leads north from Grange-in-Borrowdale to the southern edge of the long and narrow Derwent Water **(below)**, which is perfect for canoeing, kayaking, windsurfing and rowing.

⑤ Seathwaite

At the end of a country road, tiny Seathwaite is the start of hiking routes up Scafell Pike and Great Gable **(above)**. There is also a good campsite here.

⑥ Allerdale Ramble

A long-distance walk of up to 97 km (60 miles), the Allerdale Ramble runs between Seathwaite and the Solway Firth, taking in gorgeous land- and seascapes.

⑦ Stonethwaite

Lying on the Cumbria Way (see p24), Stonethwaite provides accommodation for hikers in some of its whitewashed cottages, and at the Langstrath Country Inn (see p119).

⑧ Seatoller

This pretty hamlet is a good base for fell walkers. Seatoller is also the starting point of the bizarre annual manhunt inspired by Robert Louis Stevenson's *Kidnapped*, when runners chase each other over the fells.

⑩ Grange-in-Borrowdale

The village, built around a stone bridge **(above)** over the Derwent, is an enchanting spot. Enjoy the view from the pretty Grange Bridge Cottage Teashop (see p101).

⑨ The Borrowdale Rambler

Bus No. 78, more poetically known as the Borrowdale Rambler, is a great way of touring this part of the Lakes. The route winds through Borrowdale before ending at Seatoller.

Borrowdale

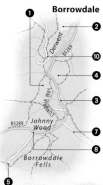

🔟 ⭐ Ambleside

Ambleside is a terrific base for a holiday in the Lakes, especially if you are not just looking for outdoor activities. It has an attractively sophisticated air for such a small place, with a couple of cinemas, cafés, bookshops and some excellent restaurants. As well as being handy for accessing the northern shores of Windermere, it is also within easy reach of Langdale *(see pp24–5)*. If you need to stock up on camping, hiking or climbing gear this is the place to do it – there are innumerable well-stocked outdoor stores here.

1 Walk to Stock Ghyll Force

The leafy path up to Stock Ghyll Force **(above)** starts behind the Salutation Hotel. It is a short, steep walk to reach the lovely waterfall, where you can find a suitable rocky outcrop on which to have a picnic.

2 Waterhead

Pretty Waterhead **(above)** is a 10-minute walk from Ambleside, on the shore of Windermere.

3 Stagshaw Gardens

These very attractive woodland gardens, 20 minutes walk south of Ambleside, are at their best in the early spring, when their abundant azaleas and rhododendrons are in full bloom.

4 Rydal Mount

Wordsworth and his family moved to Rydal Mount in 1813, and he lived here until his death in 1850. It was a much-loved family home, and the original paintings, furniture and numerous personal effects are still in situ.

NEED TO KNOW

MAP F5

Stagshaw Gardens: 015394 46402; dawn–dusk daily; adm £2.50

Rydal Mount: Rydal; 015394 33002; Mar–Oct: 9:30am–5pm daily; Nov, Dec & Feb: 11am–4pm Wed–Sun; adm £7.50

Bridge House: Apr–Oct: 11:30am–4:15

Ambleside Climbing Wall: Lake Road; 015394 33794;

10am–6:30pm Mon–Fri (to 6pm Sat & Sun); adm £7.50–8.50; taster sessions: £18

Armitt Museum: Rydal Road; 015394 31212; 10am–4:30pm Tue–Sat; adm £5

■ Parking in Ambleside is difficult and expensive, so it is easier to take a bus.

■ A visit to Zefferelli's restaurant *(see p85)* is a must for any visitor.

6 Bridge House

This high-arched picturesque little building (left) straddles Stock Beck. Built as an apple store in the 17th century, and once home to a family of eight, it is now run by the National Trust, and its simple, pretty rooms offer glimpses into local history.

RUSHBEARING

This festival centres on the church of St Mary's and is held in early July. Children parade with rush crosses, then lay them on the floor of the church. This dates back to the time when the floor was compacted earth covered with rushes (see p66).

8 Armitt Museum

This excellent local history museum also houses a Beatrix Potter exhibition, featuring her botanical drawings and delicate watercolours.

9 Ambleside Roman Fort

Set on the lakeshore, 15 minutes walk south of Ambleside, a rectangular stone outline of foundations is all that remains of this 2nd-century Roman fort. It was built as a supply depot and to protect the main road through the district.

5 St Mary's Parish Church

This fine Gothic-Revival building is the work of Sir George Gilbert Scott. It features a 1940s mural depicting the town's Rushbearing Ceremony.

7 Ambleside Climbing Wall

This five-storey building has a 10.5-m (34-ft) climbing wall (above) and a bouldering room as well. Café Altitude overlooks the wall with glass viewing panels.

10 Jenkins Crag

This stony, rocky outcrop provides a great view over Windermere and is a good hike from Waterhead. From here you can also walk to Townend (see p14) and Troutbeck (see p73).

🔟 ⭐ Langdale

Langdale is the best area in which to see the beauty and grandeur of the Lake District. More accessible than Wasdale, the valley is sculpted on a truly epic scale, with the steep, verdant fell walls giving way to even higher and sterner mountain ranges. This place is a hiker's heaven, and the attractive villages in the valley do their utmost to keep walkers fed and watered. Probably the nicest of these settlements is the riverside village of Elterwater.

3 Blea Tarn
Tranquil Blea Tarn **(above)** sits on the road between Little and Great Langdale. The Langdale Pikes are beautifully framed within the gap created by Blea Tarn Pass. Little Langdale Tarn is another nearby beauty spot that is well worth seeking out.

1 Crinkle Crags
The evocative name of Crinkle Crags **(above)** derives from the five rises and dips of this line of fells. Part of two major mountain rings, these hills are praised by Wainwright *(see p54)* in his *Pictorial Guides*.

2 High Close Estate
Established by a local merchant in the 1860s, this garden hosts a fine collection of mature North American trees. There are views over Loughrigg Tarn and Elterwater.

4 Cumbria Way
Running from Ulverston in the south to Carlisle in the north, the 113-km (70-mile) Cumbria Way cuts a scenic swathe through Langdale. You can stay at the Old Dungeon Ghyll Hotel *(see p119)* or the National Trust campsite.

Previous pages *Wast Water and Wasdale*

6 Chapel Stile

This pretty slate-quarrying village on the river Brathay **(above)** is home to one of the Lakes' most classic watering holes: Wainwrights' Inn.

5 Wrynose Pass

Featuring narrow, staggering inclines, Wrynose Pass **(below)** will give nervous drivers palpitations. However, it rewards with dramatic mountain views.

7 Elterwater

This charming village has rugged stone cottages wreathed in honeysuckle and the river Brathay running through it.

8 Skelwith Bridge

The former slate-mining village of Skelwith Bridge is set around the bridge that spans the Brathay. Visitors can still buy articles made from the blue-green slate at Chesters by the River.

9 Stickle Ghyll

The cascades of the waterfall at Stickle Ghyll are dramatic, especially after heavy rain. This forms the starting point for a steep, hour-long hike up to the tranquil, 457-m (1,500-ft) high Stickle Tarn.

10 Colwith Force

The waterfall tumbles down 12 m (40 ft) of mossy rocks edged by woodland. It can be reached via a footpath from Skelwith Bridge.

TOP 10 ⭐ Wordsworth's Lake District

William Wordsworth and the landscape of the Lakes are forever linked in the public imagination. Born in Cockermouth in 1770, Wordsworth died at Rydal Mount in 1850, and there are sites linked with him throughout the region, from pretty Dove Cottage, where he lived with his sister Dorothy and family, to Easedale Tarn, immortalized in *The Prelude*. Bring with you his *Selected Poems* and Dorothy's journals, to get a real feel of the places he adored.

1 All Saints Church, Cockermouth

Wordsworth's father, who died when William was 13, is buried in the mid-19th-century All Saints **(below)**. It also has a memorial window to Wordsworth, designed by John Hardman.

4 Rydal Mount

This relatively grand house **(right)** was Wordsworth's home in his later years. Visitors can see the poet's books, paintings, the couch on which he lay, and his summer house in the garden.

2 Dove Cottage

Built in the 17th century, Dove Cottage provides an insight into the social history of the Lakes and the spartan lives of the Wordsworths.

3 Penrith

This town was home to Wordsworth's mother, and was where the poet and his future wife went to infant school. Visitors can make a trip here to see his maternal grandparents' house.

5 Dora's Field

Heartbroken by the death of their daughter Dora at the age of 43, Wordsworth and his wife planted daffodils in her memory beneath Rydal Mount.

6 Wordsworth House, Cockermouth

Wordsworth's birthplace brilliantly evokes 18th-century life **(right)**. Kids can play with toys and help out with chores.

7 Greenhead Ghyll

The rushing mountain stream of Greenhead Ghyll features in the tragic pastoral poem "Michael". It is reached via an attractive path just east of Grasmere.

9 Hawkshead School

The busy village of Hawkshead is home to the rugged little grammar school **(left)** that the poet attended. You can still see the signature that he scored into his wooden desk.

10 St Oswald's, Grasmere

In central Grasmere, the graveyard of St Oswald's **(below)** shelters the tombs of Wordsworth and his wife Mary, three of their children who died young, his sister Dorothy, and other members of his extended family.

8 Easedale Tarn Walk

Wordsworth's favourite hike leads northwest out of Grasmere, and then climbs steeply up a stony path to reach the beautiful tarn, or mountain lake.

NEED TO KNOW

Dove Cottage: **MAP E5**; SE of Grasmere; 015394 35544; 9:30am–5pm daily (4pm in winter); adm £7.75

Rydal Mount: **MAP F5**; Ambleside; 015394 33002; Mar–Oct: 9:30am–5pm daily; Nov, Dec & Feb: 11am–4pm Wed–Sun; adm £7.50

Wordsworth House, Cockermouth: **MAP C2**; Main Street; 01900 824805; mid-Mar–Oct: 11am–4pm Sat–Thu; adm £7.50

Hawkshead School: **MAP M2**; Hawkshead; 015394 36735; Apr–Sept: 10am–1pm & 2–5pm Mon–Sat, 1–5pm Sun; Oct: 10am–1pm & 2–3:30pm Mon–Sat, Sun 1–3:30pm; adm £2.50

■ **Dove Cottage is a very popular attraction. Try going early or late in the day (or out of season) to avoid the crowds.**

■ **The Tea Room at Rydal Mount is a lovely spot with outdoor seating in the pretty gardens.**

Wordsworth's Guide to the Lakes

It is the irony of many a guidebook that the writer resents tourists thronging the area they love. Yet, in writing, they only serve to entice more visitors to the place. Such was the case with Wordsworth's *Guide to the Lakes*, first published in 1810. In spite of his misgivings, his writing described the Lakes in such a marvellous way that people were inevitably lured in vast numbers.

Literary Sites

Daffodils on the banks of Ullswater

1 Ullswater

If you time your trip to the Lakes to see "a host of golden daffodils" on the Ullswater shore (see pp88–91), spare a thought for Wordsworth's sister Dorothy. Her beautiful diary entry about the flowers inspired one of the most famous poems in the English language – "Daffodils".

2 The Fish Hotel, Buttermere
MAP C4

Broadcaster and novelist Melvyn Bragg's best-known work is *The Maid of Buttermere*, based on the real-life story of Mary Robinson, the Fish Hotel's landlord's daughter, who was seduced by a bigamist.

3 Esthwaite Water
MAP M2

To the west of Hill Top, Esthwaite Water is stocked with trout and ringed by waterlilies. The lake was an inspiration for Beatrix Potter's *The Tale of Mr Jeremy Fisher*, the story of a waistcoat-wearing frog.

4 Keswick

This was home to another literary giant – Samuel Taylor Coleridge (see p54). His fearless walks up peaks such as Scafell Pike helped to establish mountaineering as a popular activity (see pp34–5).

5 Brantwood

Home to art critic John Ruskin from 1872 until his death in 1900, Brantwood has a wonderful location above Coniston Water (see p31).

6 Ambleside

Harriet Martineau, said to be the first female journalist in England, was also renowned as a feminist, abolitionist and philosopher. She spent the latter part of her life in Ambleside (see pp20–21), residing in a house named The Knoll.

7 Hill Top

Beatrix Potter's farmhouse is 3 km (2 miles) from Windermere's western shore and is accessible via a little car ferry. Her beloved Hill Top still gives visitors a true sense of Potter's life and craft (see p15).

Beatrix Potter's writing desk, Hill Top

8 Haystacks
MAP D4

Located to the southeast of Buttermere, Haystacks was Alfred Wainwright's favourite hike – he even chose to have his ashes scattered here. He wrote of the mountain that it "stands unabashed and unashamed in the midst of a circle of much loftier fells, like a shaggy terrier in the company of foxhounds."

Nibthwaite in winter

9 Dove Cottage
Following the tenancy of the Wordsworths, Dove Cottage was occupied by the writer and intellectual Thomas de Quincey *(see p54)*, who lived here for 10 years.

10 Nibthwaite
MAP M3

A village at the southern end of Coniston Water, Nibthwaite inspired Arthur Ransome *(see p54)* to write his *Swallows and Amazons* series.

WILLIAM WORDSWORTH

Wordsworth House in Cockermouth, his birthplace, is now a fascinating living museum.

Wordsworth's poetic career was marked by his meeting with Samuel Taylor Coleridge, which resulted in the publication of the *Lyrical Ballads,* a landmark in Romantic poetry, interwoven with the ideals of the French Revolution. His other great influence was the landscape of the Lakes. Wordsworth moved here with his sister Dorothy in 1799, and immersed himself in his natural surroundings. Dorothy's observations in her journals were an inspiration for William. Many felt he had abandoned his radicalism and was past his best by the time he became Poet Laureate in 1843. *The Prelude,* the philosophical and spiritual autobiography he began in his late 1920s, is considered his greatest work.

TOP 10 EVENTS IN WORDSWORTH'S LIFE

1 He was born in Cockermouth, 1770

2 Sent to Hawkshead Grammar School after his mother died in 1778

3 Went to study at St Johns' College in Cambridge, 1787

4 Took a walking tour of Europe in 1790

5 Fell in love with Annette Vallon in the 1790s; they had a child but were separated by the French Revolution

6 Met Coleridge in 1795, and they began work on the *Lyrical Ballads* (published in 1798)

7 Moved to Dove Cottage with Dorothy in 1799

8 Married childhood friend Mary Hutchinson in 1802 – he had five children with her

9 Appointed Poet Laureate in 1843

10 Died in Cumberland in 1850 at the age of 80

Coniston Water

Coniston tends to get rather overlooked, with many visitors heading to the larger Windermere. However, Coniston's long, slender stretch of water is all the better for being less visited, with lovely attractions such as Ruskin's beautiful home, Brantwood, as well as some wonderful walks. Visitors can explore the lake on various craft, including the National Trust's 19th-century steam-powered gondola.

3 St Andrew's Church
In the village centre, don't miss this church **(left)**, where the grave of the great Victorian polymath, John Ruskin, sits beneath an impressive, Celtic-style cross.

5 Coniston Village
The copper-mining village of Coniston is a compact and engaging little place, with a couple of great pubs, including the Black Bull (see p59) and a museum.

1 Steam Yacht Gondola
This Victorian steam boat sank in a storm and spent much of the 1960s at the bottom of the lake before being rebuilt by the National Trust. It now offers cruises, including a trip to Brantwood.

2 Old Man of Coniston
It takes a couple of hours to hike from Coniston village to the Old Man, a 800 m (2,634 ft) fell with views to the coast and the Scafell Massif **(below)**.

4 Peel Island
Immortalized as Wild Cat Island in the *Swallows and Amazons* series (see p54), this tiny island **(above)** sits at the southern end of the lake.

6 Dodgson Wood
The campsite at this ancient woodland, a Site of Special Scientific Interest, is perfect for watersports and activities in Grizedale Forest.

Coniston Water

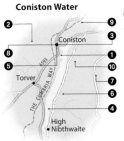

8 Ruskin Museum

This gem of a local history museum has a collection dedicated to John Ruskin. Established in 1901, the museum also has a section on racer Donald Campbell, as well as exhibits on local industries such as mining and lace-making.

9 Tarn Hows

Bequeathed to the National Trust by Beatrix Potter, Tarn Hows is one of the most famous (and most visited) beauty spots in the region.

DONALD CAMPBELL AND BLUEBIRD

Car and motorboat racer Donald Campbell was killed in an accident on Coniston Water in 1967 while he was trying to break his own world water-speed record. The boat he was racing, *Bluebird*, was recovered from the lake in 2001 and is being lovingly restored. It may take to Coniston Water again, as there is a proposal to suspend the ban on motor boats in *Bluebird's* honour.

10 Brantwood

The lovely interiors at Brantwood **(below)** feature Ruskin's collection of art and furniture. The gardens have a zigzag path imitating Dante's journey to paradise, an ancient woodland and a fern garden.

7 Grizedale Forest

This swathe of pine, oak and spruce forest features over 60 sculptures **(above)** to explore as you walk along the paths. It is also home to Go Ape treetop adventures and mountain bike trails (see p57).

NEED TO KNOW

MAP M2

Steam Yacht Gondola: 015394 32733; Apr–Oct; adm £11 half-lake cruise, £21 full-lake cruise

Dodgson Wood: 01229 885663 (campsite)

Ruskin Museum: Coniston; 015394 41164; Mar–mid-Nov: 10am–5pm daily; mid-Nov–Feb: 10:30am–3:30pm Tue–Sun; adm £6; www.ruskin museum.com

Brantwood: Coniston; 015394 41396; Mar–Nov: 10:30am–5pm daily; Nov–Mar: 10:30am–4pm Wed–Sun; adm £7.70; www.brantwood.org.uk

■ Visitors in the summer season can take a trip on the National Trust Steam Yacht Gondola.

■ Head for The Terrace, a restaurant at Brantwood, which has a lovely terrace with lake views.

🔟 ⭐ Wasdale

This valley is simply one of the wildest and most impressive places in Britain. From the village of Gosforth, a narrow road leads past lonely Wast Water and ends at the valley head with England's most mighty peaks – Scafell, Scafell Pike and Great Gable – rising before you. Pitch your tent, drop in for a pint at the venerable Wasdale Head Inn, take to the lake in a canoe, pause for contemplation in the tiny church, or just bask in the magnificent mountain views.

① Wasdale Head Inn
This is a venerable and handsome place **(below)**, and almost the only accommodation option here other than camping. For hearty meals and real ales make for cosy Ritson's Bar *(see p58)* at the inn *(see p119)*.

④ Great Gable
Pyramidal Great Gable **(below)** makes for a popular hike – it is accessible both from Wasdale and Seatoller *(see p98)*. A high pass called Windy Gap connects Great Gable to the smaller Green Gable.

② Wasdale Head
The country lane peters out into the tiny hamlet of Wasdale Head, which offers a spectacular view of a ring of soaring mountain peaks. It is quite literally the end of the road.

⑤ Canoeing on Wast Water
Only 15 canoes can access Wast Water at one time, so this stretch of chilly water, backed by scree-covered hillsides, feels all the more remote.

③ Santon Bridge
This is a quiet Lake District village beside the river Irt. There is an excellent pub here – the Bridge Inn – which hosts the idiosyncratic "World's Biggest Liar" competition every year.

Wasdale

Copeland Forest

Wasdale Head

Bleng

Nether Wasdale

Wast Water

Gosforth

A595

Mite

Santon Bridge

⑥ Mountain Biking
Little-travelled country roads and a network of rugged paths **(left)** make Wasdale an exhilarating challenge, even for the most fit and experienced mountain bikers.

⑦ Viking Cross, Gosforth

This slender 4-m (14-ft) high Viking Cross **(left)**, located in the graveyard of St Mary's in Gosforth, was carved around AD 940. It is engraved with intricate knotwork and imagery, which combines a Christian theme with Nordic figures.

LYING IN THE LAKES

The tradition of tall tales was supposedly created in Wasdale in the 19th century by publican Will Ritson. He specialized in fantastical tales – Wordsworth is said to have been one of his listeners, along with many a gullible tourist. This tradition continues with the World's Biggest Liar competition *(see p67)*, a stand-up for fibbers, held at the Bridge Inn *(see p107)*.

NEED TO KNOW

MAP D5

■ Wasdale is as wild as it looks. Do not even think about walking here without adequate gear and supplies, an Ordnance Survey map and, preferably, GPS. Tell someone where you are planning to go before you head off.

■ Wast Water is owned by the National Trust, who limit access to the lake. For details on swimming, see www.national trust.org.uk.

⑧ Scafell Pike

The highest peak in England, Scafell Pike (978 m/3,209 ft) is an enjoyable challenge, and the reward is a superb view. Keep an eye on the weather and be sure you are well kitted out *(see p113)*.

⑨ St Olaf's Church

Supposedly the smallest church in the country, St Olaf's was rebuilt in the 19th century, but there has been a church here since medieval times.

Napes Needle ⑩

For most people, just looking at the rocky spike of Napes Needle **(right)** is enough of an adrenalin boost. The ascent is only recommended for experienced climbers, as it presents a tremendous test.

Keswick

A popular and busy little town, Keswick has plenty of attractions, although it is not quite as enticing as other Lakeland settlements. Its proximity to lovely Derwent Water, however, makes it a good base for walkers and nature enthusiasts. Keswick is also a handy option for rainy days, with museums, a market, a good repertory theatre and the beautiful and historic Alhambra Cinema.

1 Moot Hall
Built in 1813, the imposing Moot Hall houses the tourist information centre and temporary exhibitions. Look out for the one-handed clock.

2 Derwent Water
Derwent Water **(above)** is dotted with wooded islands. Landing stages around the lake serve the Keswick Launch.

3 Theatre by the Lake
This beautifully sited theatre puts on a six-month summer season, as well as other shows throughout the year.

4 Keswick Museum
This museum **(above)**, housed in a Victorian Arts and Crafts building, first opened in 1898. It has retained some of its original displays, including a large set of musical stones, which you can play. There are some changing exhibitions related to the landscape and culture of Lake District.

5 Keswick Market
There has been a market in Keswick for nearly 750 years. On Thursdays and Saturdays, around the Moot Hall, up to 60 stalls sell a great range of local produce including food, crafts and clothes.

NEED TO KNOW

Moot Hall: **MAP T5**; Keswick Market Square; 017687 72645

Theatre by the Lake: **MAP S6**; 017687 74411; www.theatrebythelake.co.uk

Keswick Museum: **MAP U4**; Fitz Park, Station Road; 017687 73263; 10am–4pm daily; adm £3.50

Puzzling Place: **MAP S5**; Museum Square; 017687 775102; Nov–Mar: 11am–5pm Tue–Sun; Apr–Oct: 11am–5:30pm daily (10am–5:30pm school hols); adm £3.75; www.puzzlingplace.co.uk

Alhambra Cinema: **MAP T5**; St John's St; 017687 72195; adm £7; www.keswick-alhambra.co.uk

Derwent Pencil Museum: **MAP S4**; Southey Works, Keswick; 017687 73626; 9:30–4pm daily; adm £5.75; www.pencilmuseum.co.uk

■ The Keswick Launch is a great way to tour the lake.

■ Try the Square Orange for excellent coffee and authentic stonebaked pizzas (see p101).

6 Puzzling Place

A fascinating and fun excursion into the wonderful world of optical illusions. There are plenty of things to challenge your brain in this mind-bogglingly curious place – from the anti-gravity room to the hologram gallery, by way of interactive exhibits, artworks and sculptures.

KESWICK FESTIVALS

The array of festivals in Keswick reflects the vibrancy of this little Lakes town. There is the Keswick Film Festival in February, branded the "friendly film festival"; the literary "Words by the Water" event in March; a well-regarded international Jazz Festival in May; and a Beer Festival in June. Plus there are the usual round of agricultural fairs in summer: these generally feature an abundance of animals and are great for kids.

10 Derwent Pencil Museum

This museum **(below)** charts the history of graphite mining in the region since the Middle Ages, and 19th-century pencil production.

Keswick

8 Alhambra Cinema

This is a glamorous 1913 cinema, showing a mix of art-house and current blockbuster movies. The beautifully restored little auditorium is done up in suitably retro red velvet and white stucco.

9 Castlerigg Stone Circle

Erected around 3000 BC, this 38-stone ring **(below)** is in a lovely setting; the light on the surrounding fells provides an ever-shifting backdrop.

7 Crosthwaite

Take a stroll to the west of town to see the ancient St Kentigern church at Crosthwaite, with its languorous marble effigy of the poet Robert Southey, who is buried in the churchyard.

The Top 10
of Everything

Dramatic Castlerigg Stone Circle

TOP10 Moments in History

Neolithic stone circle at Swinside

1 3000 BC: Neolithic People

The first farmers in the Lakes area also created the atmospheric stone circle at Castlerigg *(see p35)*. Stone axes found at Scafell Pike and bronze tools at Ambleside shed some light on the lives of these early inhabitants.

2 AD 69: The Romans

The Roman presence in the Lakes is still tangible, and is associated with Hadrian's Wall, built to mark the northern limits of the British Roman Empire. The most impressive remnant is Hardknott Pass hilltop fort, which indicates the military power of the invaders.

3 AD 800–900: The Vikings

The Vikings arrived with less of a vengeance in the Lakes than in other areas. In fact, the Norse invaders were part of a wider wave of settlement, rather than arriving here bent on rape and pillage. They are remembered in many of the poetic local place names and terms.

4 The Medieval Period: Lakeland Industries

The medieval period saw the establishment of sheep-farming, as well as the beginning of a long tradition of mining. Graphite was extracted for pencil-making and glazing. Slate and copper mining also developed and gradually became integral to the local economy.

5 1300–1700: Border Raids

The Border Reivers threatened the area for more than 300 years, launching raids from the border between Scotland and England, rustling livestock, kidnapping and extorting. The distinctive "pele" towers were built as defences during this period. Many of these still stand and have formed the basis for later country houses.

6 18th and 19th Centuries: The Romantic Period

Wordsworth, Coleridge, Gainsborough, Turner and Constable were the poets and artists who immortalized the Lake District, deeply inspired by the folklore and the landscape.

Romantic poet William Wordsworth

7 1847: The Coming of the Railways

The first passenger railway line, between Kendal and Windermere was completed in 1847, and transformed the latter into a boom town. It also brought large numbers of tourists and walkers, cementing the popularity of the Lakes.

8 1895 and 1951: Conservation

These dates mark milestones in protecting the area from over-development. In 1895 the National Trust was founded; its land ownership in the area owes much to the children's author Beatrix Potter, who made large bequests to the Trust. The Lake District National Park was established in 1951 to prevent insensitive development.

Evacuations during the 2015 floods

9 2009 and 2015: Flooding

The Lake District suffered two of the worst floods in Britain's history. Cockermouth and Keswick were both completely inundated, with many buildings badly damaged. The stone bridge at Pooley Bridge was also completely destroyed in 2015 – replaced for now by a pontoon.

10 2016: National Park Expanded

The Lake District National Park was expanded by some 70 sq km (27 sq miles), with extensions added to the eastern regions. This coincided with major additions to the Yorkshire Dales. The M6 motorway is now the dividing line between the two large, contiguous National Parks.

TOP 10 PREHISTORIC AND ROMAN SITES

Ravenglass Roman Bath House

1 Long Meg and Her Daughters
MAP H2 ▪ Little Salkeld, the Eden Valley
This is a perfect circle of 69 stones, dating from around 2500 BC.

2 Mayburgh Henge
MAP G2 ▪ 3 km (2 miles) south of Penrith
This circular earthwork has a single standing stone at the centre.

3 Ravenglass Roman Bath House
MAP J2 ▪ Ravenglass
The 4-m- (13-ft-) high walls suggest the scale of this Roman bath house, which was built in AD 130.

4 Castlerigg Stone Circle
MAP E3 ▪ Near Keswick
Dating back to 3000 BC, this is among the most atmospheric sites in Britain.

5 Hardknott Roman Fort
MAP D6 ▪ Hardknott Pass
This isolated Roman fort is imposing.

6 Ambleside Roman Fort
MAP F5 ▪ Ambleside
There is little left to see of this fort, but it is a lovely verdant spot.

7 Barnscar Bronze Age Settlement
MAP K2 ▪ 5 km (3 miles) from Ravenglass
Here visitors can see moorland hut circles, cairns and field systems.

8 Swinside Stone Circle
MAP L3 ▪ Near Broughton-in-Furness
The impressive Swinside has a circle of 55 stones set in lush farmland.

9 The Langdale Boulders
MAP E5 ▪ Near Chapel Stile
This cluster of craggy, patterned rocks is a fine example of prehistoric art.

10 Rock Art, Ullswater
MAP F4
These patterns date back 5,000 years.

🔟 Museums and Galleries

1 The Beacon Museum

This imaginative, interactive museum is housed in a lighthouse-like building on the harbour. The exhibits explore Copeland's turbulent and fascinating story. There's rich background on the slave trade and smuggling, as well as an exhibition, the Sellafield Story, devoted to west Cumbria's nuclear industry. The top floor offers great views through high-powered telescopes (see p106).

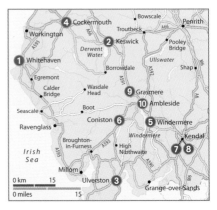

2 Keswick Museum

Founded in 1873, this museum offers a step-back-in-time experience, with a fascinating Victorian gallery of curiosities and treasures housed in traditional cases. Letters and memorabilia associated with Wordsworth and other Lakes' poets and writers, as well as exhibits on the lives of locals, are on display here (see p34).

Statues of Laurel and Hardy, in Ulverston

3 Laurel and Hardy Museum

MAP M4 ■ Brogden Street, Ulverston ■ 01229 582292 ■ Open Easter–Nov: 10am–5pm daily ■ Adm ■ www.laurel-and-hardy.co.uk

An engaging collection of memorabilia celebrates the Ulverston origins of comic star Stan Laurel. The family-run museum, housed in a former 1930s cinema, plays Stan and Ollie's slapstick movies on a loop. A statue in County Square in the town commemorates the timeless comedy duo.

4 Castlegate House Gallery

An interesting contemporary space set in a Cockermouth Georgian town house, Castlegate House focuses on paintings, prints and ceramics by 20th-century and contemporary British artists, in particular those from the north of England and southern Scotland. The works of emerging artists are showcased, as are pieces by iconic names such as Grayson Perry, Winifred Nicholson and Sheila Fell. Rare, early studio pottery is another speciality of the gallery (see p99).

Keswick Museum

5 Windermere Jetty: Museum of Boats, Steam and Stories

This magnificent collection of historic vessels includes *Dolly*, which is the oldest mechanically powered boat in the world. The exhibits on display also include dugout boats dating from between 1200 and 1320, yachts and a copper ore barge *(see pp14–15)*.

6 Ruskin Museum

A celebration of all things Ruskin-related, this museum examines John Ruskin's life as a still-influential art critic and historian, and exhibits his attractive watercolours and drawings. Local industries are also explored, and there are displays of delicate linen and lace. A whole wing is devoted to Donald Campbell and his iconic *Bluebird* hydroplane *(see p31)*.

7 Museum of Lakeland Life and Industry

Explore the history of the Lake District and its inhabitants through re-created rooms from significant periods in Lakeland life. There are also displays devoted to *Swallows and Amazons* author Arthur Ransome and to the Arts and Crafts movement in the Lake District *(see p17)*.

Museum of Lakeland Life and Industry

8 Abbot Hall Art Gallery

This gallery has a national reputation for its contemporary and historic works, and is housed in a Grade I listed villa on the banks of the river Kent. The restored Georgian

Belcamp's *The Great Picture* (1646)

interiors of the ground floor showcase an impressive collection of 18th- and 19th-century portraits and landscapes, including a comprehensive collection of George Romney's work. The gallery also hosts an ambitious temporary exhibition programme *(see p17)*.

9 Wordsworth Museum

Wordsworth's life and times are examined in absorbing detail, through letters, taped readings of his poems, portraiture and reminiscences. There is an emphasis on the rural life explored in the poet's works and entertaining detail on his domestic sphere – visitors can see his toothscrapers, lunch box and panama hat, as well as Dorothy's tiny shoes. There are regular talks, readings and other events. Dove Cottage is just next door *(see pp12–13)*.

10 The Armitt Museum

This museum is dedicated to preserving and sharing the cultural heritage of the Lake District, and its collection comprises both local-history exhibits and contemporary art. There are displays on German exile Kurt Schwitters *(see p54)*, and some fascinating Beatrix Potter *(see p72)* treasures: in 1943 Potter gave the gallery 450 of her watercolours, depicting funghi, fish and mosses. The author also left the museum first-edition copies of many of her books *(see pp20–21)*.

TOP 10 Churches and Abbeys

1 St Michael and All Angels
MAP M2 ▪ Hawkshead

Perched above Hawkshead, St Michael's was founded in 1500 and boasts a 21-m- (70-ft-) high nave with impressive pillars and painted arches. As a schoolboy, Wordsworth liked to while away time here, enjoying the sweeping views of Esthwaite Water and the Langdale pikes.

Window, St Michael and All Angels

2 Shap Abbey
MAP H4 ▪ 3 km (2 miles) W of Shap

Sitting on the banks of the Lowther, the ruins of Shap Abbey create a harmonious if slightly melancholy picture. A 16th-century tower still stands, but little remains of the 13th-century buildings – church, cloister and dormitories. The abbey was begun in the late 12th-century by a Catholic religious order called the Premonstratensians, also known as the White Canons in reference to the colour of their robes.

3 St Kentigern's
MAP D3 ▪ Crosthwaite

The origins of this church on the fringes of Keswick date back to the 4th century, with the present building dating from the 16th century. It incorporates a mosaic floor, 12th-century glass, an ancient sundial and 12 Tudor "consecration crosses" that mark the places where the bishop sprinkled holy water. The church was restored in the mid-19th-century by renowned Gothic-Revival architect George Gilbert Scott.

4 Furness Abbey
MAP L5 ▪ 3 km (2 miles) N of Barrow-in-Furness ▪ 01229 823420 ▪ Open Apr–Sep: 10am–6pm daily; Oct: 10am–5pm daily; Nov–Mar: 10am–4pm Sat & Sun; call before visiting to check hours ▪ Adm ▪ www.english-heritage.org.uk

The extensive and lovely red sandstone ruins of Furness Abbey are spread over a verdant site in what Wordsworth described in his epic poem *The Prelude* as the "vale of nightshade". The abbey, located on the outskirts of Barrow-in-Furness, was founded by the Savigniac monks. Transferred to the Cistercians in the mid-12th century, it was almost entirely destroyed during the Reformation, although some fine stonework is still intact.

Picturesque ruins of Furness Abbey

⑤ St Andrew's
MAP G3 ■ Dacre

This ancient church has plenty of treasures, including a Viking monument and four bear statues that guard each corner of the churchyard. Dating from the 12th century, the church was restored in the 15th century, and again by the Victorians.

Chancel of St Andrew's

⑥ Cartmel Priory
MAP N4 ■ Priest Lane, Cartmel ■ www.cartmelpriory.org.uk

This Augustine Priory has been a place of worship for 800 years. Many features remain from the 1400s, including the square belfry tower, the rose window and the choir stalls. There is also a 20th-century sculpture, *They Fled by Night*, by Josefina de Vasconcellos.

⑦ St Olaf's

This is England's smallest, as well as one of its most atmospheric, churches. The little interior of St Olaf's is whitewashed with heavy beams overhead that are said to have come from Viking longships. Look out for the representation of the craggy Napes Needle (a pinnacle on Great Gable) etched into one of the windows. You can also visit the graves of climbers who lost their lives in early ascents of the surrounding peaks *(see p33)*.

⑧ St James's
MAP C4 ■ Buttermere

This pretty country church sits above the picturesque village of Buttermere. The southern window of St James's is dedicated to writer and walker Alfred Wainwright. From here, you can look out at Haystacks, Wainwright's favourite Lakeland hike. There has been a chapel here since the early 16th century, but the present building was constructed in 1840.

⑨ St Catherine's
MAP K1 ■ Near Boot, Eskdale

Within walking distance of Dalegarth, at the end of the Ravenglass and Eskdale line *(see p53)*, St Catherine's dates back to the 12th century. Look out for the octagonal font, decorated with stylized marigolds, inside this plain but handsome country church.

⑩ St Martin's Church
MAP F4 ■ Ullswater

This plain yet lovely little 16th-century church sits on a quiet lane above the east shore of Ullswater; it is backed by a yew tree that may be 1,300 years old. The best approach to St Martin's is from Howtown, a stop-off point on the steamer route.

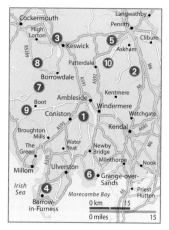

TOP 10 Castles and Houses

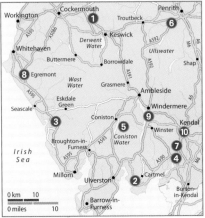

in lavish Elizabethan-Gothic style, is the only part open to the public. Visitors can explore the sumptuous library and bedrooms and climb the very grand cantilevered wooden staircase (see p74).

3 Muncaster Castle

This splendid, eccentric home has been occupied by the Pennington family since 1208. It is said to be one of Britain's most haunted castles, with much of the trouble being caused by 15th-century court jester Tom Skelton – check out his malevolent features in a large-scale portrait (see p74).

1 Mirehouse

Secluded Mirehouse features a wonderful collection of furniture, portraits and letters written by past owners to Carlyle, Tennyson and Wordsworth. Built in 1666 and sold in 1688, Mirehouse has stayed in the same family ever since (see p96).

2 Holker Hall

This imposing mansion is still home to the Cavendish family, and the west wing, built in the Victorian period

Levens Hall's lavish drawing room

4 Levens Hall

The weathered but lovely Elizabethan exterior of Levens Hall conceals a much older medieval tower. The interiors are wonderfully preserved, with their fine Italian plasterwork, leather panelling and stained glass. There is a also collection of clocks and delicate miniatures, and the topiary gardens are world famous (see p17).

5 Brantwood

John Ruskin's lakeside villa is a symphony of light and colour and a showcase for his art collection; start your visit by watching the video about

Lush gardens of Holker Hall

John Ruskin's home, Brantwood, overlooking Coniston Water

the critic and painter's life. The stunning views of Coniston are best from the Turret Room, where the aged Ruskin sat in his bath chair (see p31).

6 Dalemain

This fine house has a magnificent symmetrical Georgian façade, behind which lie intriguing Tudor and medieval buildings – in fact, the origins of this family home go back to the Saxon period. The interiors are decked out with portraits and hand-painted Oriental wallpaper, and there is also a collection of antique toys and doll houses (see p89).

7 Sizergh Castle

Constructed around a blunt medieval tower, the rambling Tudor buildings of Sizergh have been the home of the Strickland family for almost 800 years. Inside you will find ancient family portraits, Elizabethan panelling and fine French and English furniture. The castle's gardens are outstanding (see pp16–17).

8 Egremont Castle
MAP B5 ▪ Egremont

This Norman castle at Egremont sits on a mound above the little medieval market town. Although it has been in ruins since the 16th century,

Arts and Crafts chair, Blackwood

remnants of the castle's imposing walls and gatehouse give some sense of its more illustrious past.

9 Blackwell

This Arts and Crafts creation, built by M H Baillie-Scott in 1900, is wonderfully preserved, with its panelling, wall-hangings, bold stained glass and elongated furnishings intact. Blackwell also hosts historical and contemporary craft exhibitions (see p15).

10 Kendal Castle

There is no mistaking the strategic significance Kendal Castle had when it was built at the end of the 12th century – it commands an epic view over Kendal and the surrounding hills. The castle has been ruined since Tudor times, but the steep walls still give a vivid feeling of scale and power (see pp16–17).

Imposing remains of Kendal Castle

TOP 10 Gardens

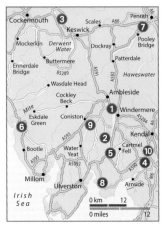

microclimate means that unusual plants such as the handkerchief tree, Chilean lantern tree and Kashmir cypress can flourish.

2 Graythwaite Hall Garden

MAP N3 ▪ Graythwaite, Ulverston ▪ 015395 31248 ▪ Open Apr–Aug: 10am–6pm daily ▪ Adm ▪ www.graythwaite.com

This late Victorian garden in a wooded valley was designed by Thomas Mawson. It is at its best in spring, when you can wander the woodland paths and see the azaleas and rhododendrons in bloom.

3 Mirehouse

This garden dates back to the late 18th century, as the mighty Scots pines along the drive testify. At the front of the house is a lovely wild flower meadow. There is also a bee garden with hives, and an orchard of Cumbrian fruit trees (see p96).

4 Levens Hall

In the grounds of Elizabethan Levens Hall, this flamboyant topiary garden was created in 1694. Other historic elements in the garden include a nuttery (see p17).

1 Brockhole Gardens

MAP N1 ▪ Brockhole, Windermere ▪ 015394 46601 ▪ Open 9am–dusk daily ▪ www.brockhole.co.uk

This lovely Arts & Crafts garden is structured with terraces that look towards Windermere and the Langdale Pikes. It features old-fashioned roses, a wild flower meadow, a kitchen garden and herbaceous borders. A mild

Levens Hall's magnificent topiary gardens

View of Windermere from Fell Foot

5 Fell Foot

A beautiful Victorian park sloping down to Windermere, Fell Foot is awash with daffodils in spring. The crenellated boathouse here adds architectural interest. Get a different perspective on the park by renting a rowing boat and exploring the lake *(see pp14–15)*.

6 Muncaster Castle

A stroll down the driveway of Muncaster Castle has an *Alice in Wonderland* feel: visitors are dwarfed by the enormous hardwood trees, planted in the late 18th century. Visit in April and May to see the similarly monumental rhododendrons and azaleas of the Sino-Himalayan gardens in flower; there is also a collection of magnolias, camellias and maples *(see p74)*.

7 Children's Garden, Dalemain

MAP G3 ▪ Dalemain ▪ 017684 86450 ▪ Open Apr–Oct: 10:30am–5pm Sun–Thu (Jun & Jul: also 10am–4:30pm Fri) ▪ Adm ▪ www.dalemain.com

Dalemain's symmetrical pink ashlar façade is softened by tall clusters of herbaceous plants. Explore a little further and find hidden treasures for children including a topiary dragon and bed of animal-and bird-named plants, such as squirrel-grass and cranesbill. A large mound of earth resembles a sleeping giant, and hard-carved wooden animals live among the plants.

8 Holker Hall

The gardens at Holker Hall beautifully combine structured and formal elements, such as the long, stepped water cascades with patches of ancient woodland. One of the great treasures of the grounds is the 16th-century Great Holker Lime which, with an 8-m (26-ft) girth, is one of the oldest and biggest lime trees in the country *(see p74)*.

9 Brantwood

Many elements of the wonderfully imaginative gardens at Brantwood were the creation of John Ruskin himself. The Zig-Zaggy, for example, was structured to depict Dante's journey to paradise, while Ruskin's favourite, the Professor's Garden, has plants that benefit both body and soul *(see p31)*.

Rock garden at Sizergh Castle

10 Sizergh Castle

The spacious and romantic gardens at Sizergh, surrounded by ancient woodland, feature orchards and a magnificent limestone rock garden, as well as stretches that are carpeted with wild flowers, a water garden and an impressive collection of ferns *(see pp16–17)*.

Walks

1 Ambleside to Skelwith Bridge

MAP N1–M1

This lovely route is a good starter before you attempt more demanding Lakeland hikes. Suitable for people of all ages, it winds its way from Ambleside via Loughrigg Tarn to Skelwith Bridge, which is a good place to stop for a pint of beer. All along the way, the Langdale Pikes provide a magnificent backdrop.

Distant peaks of Crinkle Crags

2 Crinkle Crags

The profile of these peaks forms five distinct "crinkles", which make for a pretty strenuous hike *(see p24)*. This trek is best attempted on a clear day, both for the views and for safety. The vast majority of walkers start their ascent from the Old Dungeon Ghyll Hotel *(see p119)*.

3 Grizedale Forest

Located on the eastern shores of Coniston Water, Grizedale Forest comprises 24 sq km (9 sq miles) of larch, oak, spruce and pine woodland. A haven for red deer and roe deer, this forest also features a terrific sculpture trail with works created by well-known British artists such as Andy Goldsworthy and David Nash. The walking routes are marked with specific colour codes *(see p31)*.

4 Coffin Trail

This rather grim-sounding route was taken by coffin bearers shouldering their load across the hills to St Oswald's in Grasmere for burial. The woodland paths link Grasmere with Rydal and on to Ambleside, and make for a secluded and not-too-demanding hike *(see p12)*.

5 Aira Force

A steep, lovely and fairly short walk from the shores of Ullswater leads up to the magnificent 20-m (65-ft) drop of Aira Force waterfall. Visitors may spot red squirrels among the attractive woodland paths here. There is also a tearoom at hand, with fine views *(see p91)*.

6 Scafell Pike

The highest mountain in England, Scafell Pike can be approached from various directions such as Wasdale, Seathwaite Farm in Borrowdale or the Old Dungeon Ghyll Hotel. Make sure you are equipped for the trek *(see p33)*.

7 Old Man of Coniston

Walking guru Wainwright wrote about the slate mines scarring the Old Man of Coniston, and visitors can still see the remnants of these mining works here. The mountain has spectacular views out over Coniston Water, and its well-worn trails make it a favourite with hikers *(see p30)*.

View from the Old Man of Coniston

Hikers on Striding Edge, Helvellyn

8 Helvellyn

As England's third-highest peak, Helvellyn should not be approached lightly. The narrow Striding Edge route is a challenging scramble, only for experienced and well-equipped hikers. Wordsworth, who climbed this mountain regularly, wrote of the death of a walker in an attempt on Striding Edge (see p90).

9 Great Gable

One of the region's iconic climbs, Great Gable has a distinctive pyramidal peak. On a clear day, the summit offers stunning views of Wasdale, Scafell and Scafell Pike. A classic route up the mountain is via Seathwaite (see p103).

10 Easedale Tarn

Hike from Grasmere up the fellsides to Easedale Tarn, a lake that sits among some forbidding peaks. A round trip takes about three hours, and the ascent is pretty steep, but it is wonderfully peaceful (see p82).

TOP 10 THINGS TO PACK

Selection of sturdy walking boots

1 Good walking boots
Tough, waterpoof boots, providing a strong grip and ankle support, are essential for any hikes in the region.

2 Outdoor clothing
It's essential to wear weatherproof and warm clothing, whatever the conditions are like when you start out.

3 Map
Bring along a good, detailed map of your planned route – as well as someone who is able to read it.

4 GPS and compass
As with a map, you should also take with you a GPS (and compass for backup), and know how to use them.

5 Whistle and mirror
If you get stuck, a whistle and mirror can help attract the attention of other hikers or rescue services.

6 Torch and spare batteries
Useful if you unexpectedly find yourself out after dark, a torch can also be used to signal in emergencies.

7 Toilet paper
This is essential, but often forgotten. Bury any degradable waste well away from paths and water sources.

8 Food and water
Always pack at least a bottle of water and a snack – such as the famous local energy bar, Kendal Mint Cake.

9 Binoculars
These are useful for bird-watching, as well as for scouting out the route or just for admiring the views.

10 Camera/mobile
There might not be a good reception in the region, but a mobile phone is still useful to bring with you for its camera.

🔟 Swims

Competitors in the Great North Swim

① Great North Swim
MAP N1 ■ Windermere
■ www.greatswim.org

This terrific communal event has four courses of open-water swimming in Windermere. You are likely to be splashing alongside 6,000 others – there is an elite course for the pros, but swimmers of all abilities can join in. It takes place in summer or early autumn, and balmy temperatures are not guaranteed.

② Silecroft Beach
MAP K4

Tucked away in the south of the Lake District, this is a lovely sand and shingle beach backed by Black Combe. Silecroft beach is great for a paddle and a swim, as well as for wind-surfing, water-skiing, canoeing and a spot of sea-fishing.

③ High Dam
MAP M3 ■ Finsthwaite

This deep tarn, which once powered the Stott Park Bobbin Mill *(see p15)*, is a peaceful place for a scenic swim. Surrounded by larches and Scots pine, High Dam is located near the village of Finsthwaite, and reached on a footpath from the Lake District National Park (LDNP) car park, passing Low Dam on route.

④ River Esk, Eskdale
MAP C6

The course of the river Esk, framed by stone bridges, is punctuated by natural pools that are perfect for a swim on the rare but magical hot days in the Lakes. You can also fish here, and it is possible to hire a canoe to tackle parts of the river.

⑤ Rydal Water
Take a dip among the reed beds of Rydal Water, beloved of Wordsworth. The mountain views in this part of the Central Fells are unbeatable and make the swim truly memorable *(see p82)*.

Rydal Water, perfect for a wild swim

St Bees' picturesque sandy beach

6 St Bees

South of Whitehaven, St Bees features a wonderful long sandy beach, divided by wooden groynes. It is edged by St Bees Head, 6 km (4 miles) of red sandstone cliffs with colonies of puffins, razorbills and guillemots. The name derives from the 9th-century St Bega, to whom a priory here was dedicated after the Norman Conquest *(see p102)*.

7 Peel Island, Coniston
MAP M3

Follow in the adventurous footsteps of Arthur Ransome's *Swallows and Amazons* brigade *(see p54)* and paddle a canoe out to Peel Island – known as Wild Cat Island in the books – for a swim in the cove in the chilly Coniston Water.

8 Beacon Tarn
MAP L3

The tucked-away Beacon Tarn provides an outdoor swim for romantics, along with sweeping views of Coniston Water. Reachable only on foot, the tarn, which is thought to be the warmest swim in the Lakes, is located near the southern end of Coniston Water. Visitors can park in the Brown Howe car park for the relatively short walk to reach the tarn.

9 Blackmoss Pot
MAP D4 ■ Stonethwaite

This deep natural pool is edged by high rocks, from which fearless swimmers love to jump. With a waterfall at each end, Blackmoss Pot is the perfect spot for a long summer wallow after a hike in Borrowdale. Its secluded location also makes it a popular choice for skinny-dipping.

10 Wast Water

Brace yourself for some deep waters and for truly impressive views of the surrounding scree-covered slopes. Wast Water is 5 km (3 miles) long, so it provides a really stretching challenge for strong swimmers *(see p104)*. Warm up with hearty pub grub at the Wasdale Head Inn *(see p119)*.

Bracing Wast Water

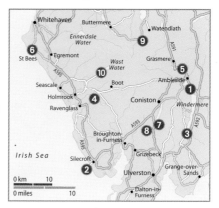

Great Journeys

① Blea Tarn Road

This road enables you to do a 13-km (8-mile) circuit of Great and Little Langdale, one of the most scenic areas in the Lake District, with plenty of beautiful ghylls and tarns. Break your journey at Old Dungeon Ghyll where you can enjoy a walk as well as relax over a pint of local real ale and lunch at the Old Dungeon Ghyll Hotel *(see p119)*.

② Coniston Cruise

MAP M2 ▪ Coniston ▪ 01768 77575 ▪ Feb–Oct: daily; Nov–Jan: Sat & Sun ▪ Adm ▪ www.conistonlaunch. co.uk

Take a trip in *Swallows and Amazons* country with the Coniston Launch service. It runs leisurely cruises plus scheduled services for a quick but enjoyable trip across the lake.

③ Kirkstone Pass

MAP F5

This spectacular white-knuckle drive in the Lakes, between Ambleside and Patterdale, offers superb views in each direction. However, the steep gradients of this high pass make it tough going in bad weather. Take a break at the rambling, whitewashed Kirkstone Pass Inn *(see p84)*.

Driving the testing Hardknott Pass

④ Hardknott Pass

The name conveys something of the gritty adventure that driving on this steep road entails *(see p80)*. The route links the two valleys of Eskdale and Langdale, but is definitely more of a gear-grinding challenge rather than a short cut. Stop to see the impressive remains of the Hardknott Roman Fort, built in the 2nd century under Emperor Hadrian *(see p39)*.

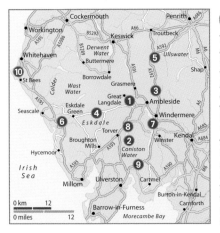

⑤ Ullswater Steamer

These elegant boats are an essential part of the Ullswater landscape. The fleet includes *Lady of the Lake*, believed to be the oldest working passenger vessel in the world – it has been operating since 1877 – and the *Raven*, which took to the water in 1889. These converted steamers connect up Glenridding in the south with Howtown, the halfway point, and the village of Pooley Bridge in the north *(see p88)*.

Ravenglass and Eskdale Railway

MAP J2–K2 ■ Ravenglass ■ 01229 717171 ■ www.ravenglass-railway.co.uk

Built to carry iron ore, this heritage steam-railway line follows a scenic route from the coast into spectacular Eskdale. Starting from Ravenglass in the west, it trundles its way to Dalegarth via the base of Muncaster Fell and Eskdale Green. Stop at Ravenglass to visit the fascinating museum.

7 Windermere Cruises

All kinds of ferries ply the lake, with stops at Waterhead, Bowness and Lakeside. Take the Jazz Buffet Cruise with live performances by the Trickle Change jazz band for a laid-back Lakes experience. Additionally, a small car ferry carries visitors straight across the lake from Bowness to Far Sawrey (see p15).

8 Steam Yacht Gondola

Take a trip on this elegant little pleasure steamer up Coniston Water. The 90-minute Explorer Cruise includes a commentary on writer Arthur Ransome and art critic and social thinker John Ruskin. The 11am Ruskin Experience Cruise (Sun–Fri) makes a stop at Ruskin's home (see p31) and the Gothic country house Monk Coniston (see pp30–31).

Steam Yacht Gondola on Coniston

Lakeside & Haverthwaite steam train

9 Lakeside & Haverthwaite Railway

This picturesque little branch line makes a 6-km (4-mile) journey to link the village of Haverthwaite with the southern end of Windermere. Here you can leave the train and continue your leisurely journey on the water (see pp14–15).

10 Cumbrian Coast Line

www.cumbriancoastline.co.uk

A little off the tourist trail, the Cumbrian Coast railway line visits intriguing destinations such Barrow-in-Furness, Millom, Ravenglass, St Bees and Whitehaven. The journey ends at Carlisle, where visitors can link up with mainline services.

Writers and Artists

Thomas de Quincey

The guides at Dove Cottage *(see p12)* make valiant efforts to tell the story of the building's second-most famous inhabitant, Thomas de Quincey. The author of *Confessions of an English Opium Eater* was drawn to the region by his adoration of Wordsworth, and lived in Dove Cottage for 10 years after the Wordsworths moved on.

Lake poet Coleridge

2 Samuel Taylor Coleridge

Coleridge, along with his friend Wordsworth, was a founder of the English Romantic movement. The Romanticism of these poets was inseparable from the transcendent beauty of the Lakes. Coleridge immersed himself in the landscape, taking long and daring hikes, which ultimately helped to establish climbing as a leisure pursuit.

3 Alfred Wainwright

Walker, author and alleged curmudgeon, Wainwright is an inescapable presence in the Lake District, more than 25 years after his death. His monument is the seven-volume illustrated guide that still serves as an invaluable point of reference to local fell walkers.

4 Beatrix Potter

Characters such as Peter Rabbit and Jeremy Fisher need no introduction for generations of children. The independence of their creator, Beatrix Potter, was hard-won, as her parents were unsympathetic to her literary ambitions. Eventually, Potter's success enabled her to buy her home at Hill Top *(see p15)*.

5 Kurt Schwitters

Born in Hanover in 1887, Kurt Schwitters made the Lakes his home after he was branded a degenerate artist by the Nazis. He is known for his collages made from discarded materials – called *Merz Pictures* – examples of which can be seen at the Armitt Museum in Ambleside *(see pp20–21)*.

6 Arthur Ransome

Ransome authored the perennial favourite, *Swallows and Amazons*, tales of childhood derring-do that were inspired by his holidays in Coniston. Ransome was also a journalist and foreign correspondent with a strong interest in Russia; his second wife was Trotsky's secretary.

7 J M W Turner

The changing light on the mountains of the Lake District was a perfect subject for Turner, who visited the region in the late

Turner's view of Buttermere

18th century. His image of stormy Buttermere can be seen at Tate Britain in London.

(8) Dorothy Wordsworth

Much has been written about Dorothy's closeness to her brother William, focusing on her strained account of his wedding to Mary. The truth of their relationship is unknown, but Dorothy's own observations of nature and of a vanished rural way of life are a must-read for visitors.

Lady Hamilton, painted by Romney

(9) George Romney

Born in Dalton-in-Furness in 1734, Romney trained as a painter in Kendal before setting up as a society artist in London; he painted many portraits of Lady Emma Hamilton, the mistress of Lord Nelson. Fans of Romney's fluid and sensual portraits should make a beeline for the Abbot Hall Art Gallery in Kendal (see p17).

(10) William Wordsworth

Wordsworth's evocations of the Lake District's monumental splendour firmly placed the area on the tourist map, and continue to draw visitors today. The Selected Poems are a good introduction to his writing, and visits to Dove Cottage and Rydal Mount tell you much about the man himself (see pp26–9).

TOP 10 BOOKS SET IN THE LAKES

Shepherd-author James Rebanks

1 The Shepherd's Life (James Rebanks)
A fascinating account of modern rural life in a remote part of the fells.

2 The Lake District Series (Martin Edwards)
Dark crime thrillers set in the Lakes.

3 All Quiet on the Orient Express (Magnus Mills)
A sinister but darkly comic tale of a bemused Lakes' visitor trying his best to fit in with the locals.

4 The Maid of Buttermere (Melvyn Bragg)
Based on the true story of an innkeeper's beautiful daughter (see p28), who is seduced by a bigamist.

5 The Grasmere Journals (Dorothy Wordsworth)
A record of life at Dove Cottage, with lyrical observations of the Lakes.

6 Rogue Herries (Hugh Walpole)
A passionate romance set in 18th-century Cumberland.

7 Unruly Times (A S Byatt)
Byatt explores the relationship between the two great poets, Wordsworth and Coleridge.

8 Swallows and Amazons (Arthur Ransome)
Written in 1930, this classic children's adventure is set in the Lake District.

9 Recollections of the Lake Poets (Thomas de Quincey)
De Quincy's candid biographical essays on the Lakes' literary titans.

10 Postman Pat (John Cunliffe)
The enchanting tales of a Lake District postman and his black-and-white cat.

Children's Attractions

Boating on Windermere at Fell Foot

1 Fell Foot

This park has expansive grounds in which to stroll, play games and have picnics. There is also an adventure playground for children. The castellated boathouse on the shores of Windermere rents out rowing boats and kayaks, and also serves as a café and shop *(see pp14–15)*.

2 Ullswater Steamer

There are plenty of options for lake-bound trips, but the Ullswater Steamers, with their picture-book scarlet funnels, are particularly appealing for children. Download activity sheets from the website to increase the educational value of your outing *(see p88)*.

3 Ravenglass and Eskdale Railway

Nothing thrills most small children more than a ride on a steam train. Adults are also catered for on this journey by the magnificent scenery through which the miniature loco-motives trundle, from Ravenglass on the coast to Dalegarth in the middle of mighty Eskdale *(see p53)*.

4 Lakeland Climbing Centre

Before your offspring are tempted by real-life crags, get them in train-ing at this well-run indoor centre with its great range of climbing walls and routes, a cave area and bouldering rooms. It runs 90-minute taster sessions, more involved classes and outdoor trips, too *(see pp16–17)*.

5 Brockhole, the Lake District Visitor Centre

MAP N2 ▪ 015394 46601 ▪ Open 10am–5pm daily (Nov–Mar: to 4pm) ▪ www.brockhole.co.uk

The visitor centre in Windermere has an adventure playground complete with a treetop trek, an indoor soft play area, mini-golf, boat rentals and lots of events geared towards children.

Families board the Ullswater Steamer

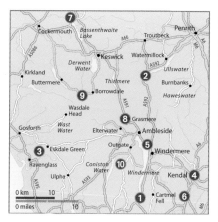

Milking at Low Sizergh Barn

The second-storey café at Sizergh looks down at the milking shed, where you can see the herd ambling in for milking each afternoon. This, and the farm trail with its chicks, sheep, cows and ancient woodland, all contribute to an educational yet irresistible children's outing (see pp16–17).

Lake District Wildlife Park

MAP D2 ■ Bassenthwaite ■ 017687 76239 ■ Open 10am–5:30pm daily ■ Adm ■ www.lakedistrictwildlife park.co.uk

This 24-acre (10-ha) site is home to more than 100 species, including meerkats, lemurs and zebras. The regular bird of prey flying displays are a popular feature, and hands-on wildlife experiences enable visitors to get up close and personal with some of the appealing animals.

Allan Bank

MAP E5 ■ Grasmere ■ 015394 35143 ■ Open Apr–Oct: 10am–5pm daily; Nov–Dec: 10am–4pm Fri–Sun ■ Adm ■ www.nationaltrust.org.uk

This is an ideal spot for children to explore and play. Look out for red squirrels on the woodland trail and build your own den or have a picnic in the grounds. There is also a playroom with board games and a craft room.

Honister Slate Mine

MAP D4 ■ Honister Pass, between Buttermere and Borrowdale ■ 017687 77230 ■ Tours: 10:30am, 12:30pm & 3:30pm daily ■ Adm ■ www.honister.com

Located at the summit of the steep Honister Pass, the slate mine offers underground tours that are an eye-opener for kids – they can learn how young children laboured in the mine in times gone by. The drive to get here is an adventure in itself, and children over ten years of age can also climb their way around the mine using the Via Ferrata grips, rails and cables.

Young visitors to Honister Slate Mine

Go Ape

MAP M2 ■ Grizedale Forest ■ 0845 6439215 ■ Open Apr–Oct: Wed–Mon; Nov & Feb: Sat & Sun ■ Adm ■ www.goape.co.uk

A challenging, not to say slightly scary, system of zip wires, ladders, swings and platforms takes you high above the ground and through the tree canopy. There is a minimum age of six, and height restrictions also apply. Back on the ground, striking wooden sculptures dot the forest.

Pubs and Inns

① Bar at the Kings Arms Hotel, Hawkshead

A venerable Lake District Inn, in the wonderfully preserved village of Hawkshead, the Kings Arms is 500 years old, but has been sensitively modernized. There are eight cosy rooms if you fancy staying over. Real ales, malt whiskies and a beer garden complete the picture (see p76).

② Cuckoo Brow Inn, Far Sawry

From this quiet Lake District inn in an old stable block, it is only a short walk to the famous home that once belonged to Beatrix Potter and is now run by the National Trust. Hearty food is served in the cosy bar, and ales are from local breweries, including Coniston Brewery and Cumbrian Legendary Ales. Guests can explore the historical features of the inn (see p76).

③ Eagle & Child Inn, Staveley

Set on the banks of the river Kent, this lovely village inn has a large garden and is a great stop for walkers along the Kent. The list of real ales is impressive, and there are five snug bedrooms (see p76).

The Masons Arms' garden with a view

④ The Masons Arms, Cartmel Fell

The atmospheric Masons Arms offers glorious views over Winster valley from its garden. It also has draught ales and a huge range of bottled beers. The imaginative food makes good use of seasonal and local produce (see p76).

Sign for Ritson's Bar, Wasdale Head Inn

⑤ Ritson's Bar, Wasdale Head Inn

A typical Lakeland walkers' bar, located in the lovely Wasdale, Ritson's is traditional and welcoming. The filling bar meals and real ales will revive you after a hike. There are cheerful log stoves in winter and outdoor tables by a little stream in summer (see p119).

⑥ Sun Inn, Crook

A fine old whitewashed pub, the Sun Inn is located in a row of 18th-century millworkers' cottages. It features the requisite open fires and stone floors, as well as tasty traditional Lakeland food and local beers and ales (see p76).

⑦ Watermill Inn, Ings

This is an award-winning pub with a microbrewery that produces Collie Wobbles, amongst numerous other fine ales. The owners also pride themselves on their dog-friendliness (see p76).

Characterful bar of the Eagle & Child

8 Black Bull, Coniston

A 400-year-old coaching inn located under the iconic Old Man of Coniston, the Black Bull has a rich history. De Quincey stopped here en route to meeting Wordsworth, and it has also hosted Coleridge and Turner. It serves home-brewed ales, including award-winning Bluebird Bitter, Winter Warmer Blacksmiths Ale and Old Man Ale (see p76).

9 Hole in t'Wall, Bowness-on-Windermere

Pints have been served at this characterful old place, a short walk from Windermere, since 1612. The very Cumbrian name derives from the fact that a past landlord used to hand beer through a hole in the wall to his neighbour, the blacksmith (see p76).

Historic Hole in t'Wall pub

10 Hikers' Bar, Old Dungeon Ghyll Hotel

At this rugged bar converted from cow sheds muddy boots will not keep you from crossing the threshold. There are open fires in winter and a stone terrace for the summers. Real ales, Scotch whiskies and large restorative portions of pub grub are served here, and the fell-foot location is superb (see p119).

TOP 10 BREWERIES

Hawkshead Brewery's beer hall

1 Ennerdale Brewery
MAP B4 ▪ 01946 861755 ▪ Croasdale Farm, Ennerdale
This brewery makes craft natural ales.

2 Jennings Castle Brewery
MAP C2 ▪ 0845 1297185 ▪ Brewery Lane, Cockermouth
This 19th-century brewery uses water from its own well in its beers.

3 Hardknott Brewery
MAP K4 ▪ 01229 779309 ▪ Millom
A great artisanal micro-brewery.

4 Ulverston Brewing Company
MAP M4 ▪ 01229 586870 ▪ Lightburn Road, Ulverston
This award-winning micro-brewery makes Cumbria's Laurel & Hardy beers.

5 Keswick Brewing Company
The names of these craft ales all come with the prefix "Thirst" (see p62).

6 Hawkshead Brewery
This brewery produces the Hawkshead Bitter and Lakeland Gold (see p76).

7 Cumbrian Legendary Ales
MAP M2 ▪ 01539 436436 ▪ Old Hall Brewery, Hawkshead
Their bottled ales include Loweswater Gold and rich Grasmoor Dark Ale.

8 Coniston Brewing Company
MAP M2 ▪ 015394 41133 ▪ Coppermines Road, Coniston
Cask-conditioned, award-winning ales are created behind the Black Bull Inn.

9 Barngates Brewery
MAP F5 ▪ 015394 36575 ▪ Barngates, Ambleside
Soft, peaty water from a nearby tarn is used in the production of the ales.

10 Tirril Brewery
MAP H3 ▪ 01768 361846 ▪ Red House Barn, Appleby-in-Westmorland
This brewery produces ales for many pubs, including Bitter End (see p100).

Restaurants

1 L'Enclume
Simon Rogan's L'Enclume, a marvellous two-Michelin-starred restaurant in the southern Lakes, uses local wild produce and ingredients from its own farm. Housed in a former village smithy, it serves food that is innovative and masterfully presented, with a fresh, vibrant flavour provided by herbs, roots and flowers *(see p77)*.

Appetizer at L'Enclume

4 Miller Howe
Located in the luxurious Windermere hotel with fabulous views of the lake, Miller Howe offers elegant main courses such as saddle of lamb, feather blade of beef and delicious fillet of halibut. There is also a traditional afternoon tea and plenty of mouthwatering desserts *(see p77)*.

Jumble Room's bright interior

2 Jumble Room
This lively little restaurant brings a dash of style and colour to Grasmere. Blues and jazz music drifts through the restaurant. The menu is international, but they are also famous for their beer-battered fish and hand-cut chips, served with mushy peas *(see p85)*.

3 The Hazelmere
This Edwardian building, complete with frilly cast-iron trellis and street awning, is the perfect place for breakfast or afternoon tea. Counters groan under the weight of freshly baked cakes and breads, and there's a fine range of Chinese teas, too *(see p77)*.

5 Quince & Medlar
Dine by candlelight in this historic Georgian building with lovely wood panelling, where the menu features superb vegetarian food. The restaurant uses only local and seasonal ingredients to create dishes such as rosemary and cheese muffins with sundried tomato tapanade or butternut squash stack layered with spiced ginger and cumin quinoa followed by quince cheesecake *(see p101)*.

6 Drunken Duck
This terrific inn just north of Hawkshead has a warm, informal ambience. Their restaurant serves excellent and imaginative food, with a strong emphasis on meat and game. Enjoy home-brewed ales along with specialities such as pork belly and faggot with mash, king cabbage and apple *(see p77)*.

Charming exterior of the Drunken Duck Inn

7 The Samling

Awarded a Michelin Star in 2017, this celebrated, adventurous hotel-restaurant sources many ingredients direct from its own kitchen garden and livestock. Should the pricey à la carte evening menu deter you, try containing the damage slightly with the moderate set-price lunch, or even the generous and delicious afternoon tea (see p77).

Dining room of Old Stamp House

8 Old Stamp House

Award-winning chef Ryan Blackburn cooks up an adventurous menu in the Ambleside building where William Wordsworth served as the local stampmaster, collecting taxes. The specialities include local seafood and Herdwick meat. Try the succulent Yew Tree Farm herdwick hogget with artichoke, wild garlic and salsify. An multi-course tasting menu is also available, and it's quite a bargain at lunchtime (see p85).

9 The Brown Horse Inn

A fine roadside inn, The Brown Horse serves up exceptional pub food, with ingredients sourced from their own farm or within a 5-km (3-mile) radius. Try their delicious Cumbrian fell-bred lamb or loin of Winster venison. Good ales and wines accompany the food (see p77).

10 Hrishi, Gilpin Hotel & Lake House

The dining room at this rural retreat serves superb food. Try the pancetta-wrapped confit lamb shoulder with baby aubergine, asparagus, cucumber and masala sauce (see p77).

TOP 10 CULINARY SPECIALITIES

1 Grasmere Gingerbread
Grasmere's special gingerbread is made to a secret recipe and enticingly wrapped in traditional packaging.

2 Sticky Toffee Pudding
Taste this irresistibly sweet confection in its reputed birthplace, Cartmel.

3 Herdwick Lamb and Mutton
Do try the locally reared lamb and mutton, which are seasonal features of menus in the Lakes.

4 Lakes Ice Cream
MAP C4 ▪ Syke Farm, Buttermere
There are a few excellent outlets for homemade ice cream. Possibly the best is available at Syke farm.

5 Kendal Mint Cake
Dense and tooth-meltingly sweet, Kendal Mint Cake is used by walkers as an instant energy-booster (see p17).

6 Kendal Cheeses
Low Sizergh Barn (see pp16–17) is a good place at which to source superb locally produced farmhouse cheeses.

7 Cumberland Sausage
These tasty pork sausages are cooked in a coil and served whole on the plate.

8 Morecambe Bay Potted Shrimps
Local shrimps are boiled in butter with spices, then sealed with butter and packed tightly into pots.

9 Hawkshead Relish
Handmade in the village where Wordsworth went to school (see p27), these relishes have no additives: red onion marmalade is the best seller.

10 Damson Gin and Jam
Damson gin and jam, both made from fruit picked in the Lyth Valley, make extremely welcome gifts.

Slabs of Kendal Mint Cake

🔟 Places to Shop

Selling gingerbread at Sarah Nelson's

3 Castlegate House Gallery

The experience of visiting this gallery is like visiting someone's home: a beautiful, light-filled Georgian one. The walls are hung with art – there is a specialism in northern English and Scottish artists such as Sheila Fell, Percy Kelly and Winifred Nicholson (see p40 & p99).

4 Sutton's Bookshop

MAP M4 ■ 48 Market Street, Ulverston ■ 01229 588858

This 200-year-old building is full of nooks and crannies packed with an eclectic choice of new and used books, including local titles.

1 Sarah Nelson's Gingerbread Shop

Gingerbread is made to a secret recipe in this tiny whitewashed building alongside Grasmere church. The pretty blue-and-white packaging of the biscuits make them a good gift. You can also buy traditional rum butter here (see p13).

5 Kentmere Pottery

A long-established studio set alongside a 13th-century mill, Kentmere Pottery produces exquisite hand-fired and decorated ceramics (see p75).

Kentmere Pottery's ceramic sign

6 The Gallery, Yew Tree Barn

A historic barn houses a cornucopia of gifts, from Lakeland furniture to handmade ceramics and bold jewellery. Visitors can meet the artists and take a break from browsing and buying for coffee or a snack at Harry's Café Bar (see p75).

2 Keswick Brewing Company

MAP T4 ■ The Old Brewery, Brewery Lane, Keswick ■ 017687 80700 ■ www.keswickbrewery.co.uk

High-quality cask and bottled ales are created by combining traditional and modern ingredients at this historic craft brewery. Visitors can take a tour of the brewery and peruse the bottles of bitters and pale ales. The brewery also produces a great seasonal range of ales, including a malty Christmas ale that makes a good alternative festive gift.

Harry's Café Bar at Yew Tree Barn

7 Plumgarths Farm Shop

MAP P3 ▪ Lakelands Food Park, Kendal ▪ 01539 736300 ▪ Open 9am–5pm Mon–Sat, 10am–4pm Sun

This excellent shop specializes in meat produced on small Cumbrian farms, as well as a wide range of local beers, jams and relishes. Give the award-winning sausages a try.

8 Hawkshead Relish Company

This family-run company in pretty Hawkshead uses the very best of fine local ingredients to produce pickles, chutneys, preserves, jams, relishes and – their best seller – red onion marmalade, which goes well with Cumberland sausages (see p75).

Hawkshead Relish Company's store

9 Honister Slate Mine Shop

Take the rugged road to Honister and follow up a tour of the slate mine with a visit to the onsite shop. You will find a range of products fashioned out of slate, from coffee tables to clocks and placemats. You can also order personalized house signs (see p99).

10 Low Sizergh Barn

The wonderful timbered barn building with its weathered beams is home to an excellent farm shop, selling their own produce plus the best of Lakeland meats, preserves and baked goods. They also sell a range of clothes, local pottery, carpets, gardening equipment and handmade soaps (see pp16–17).

TOP 10 THINGS TO BUY

Locally brewed beers on draught

1 Pottery
Locally made pottery is a Lake District speciality, and makes a fine souvenir.

2 Paintings and Drawings
Independent galleries sell beautiful artworks depicting the fells and lakes.

3 Photographs
Epic landscapes and changing light make the Lakes really photogenic; many galleries stock prints.

4 Farm Foods
Cumberland sausages, jam, relish, cheese, bread and cake: the local produce of the Lakes is first-rate.

5 Beer
Microbreweries abound in this region, offering a wealth of delicious, unique and often quirkily named ales.

6 Slate
Handpainted signs, bird baths and sundials in dark grey slate are some typical Lakeland souvenirs.

7 Books and Maps
Local fiction, fauna, history, walks and topography – the many bookshops in the region have plenty to offer.

8 Ice Cream
Imaginative flavours and local organic ingredients make Lakeland ice cream a treat worth buying in bulk.

9 Crystal
MAP M4 ▪ 01229 584400 ▪ Oubas Hill, Ulverston
Watch crystal being made at the Lakes Glass Centre in Ulverston and then buy some at the on-site factory shop.

10 Damson Gin
Damson plums harvested in the Lyth Valley are distilled into a delicious ruby-red liqueur after having been macerated in a gin-and-sugar syrup.

🔟 Lake District for Free

Cycling through the Lake District

1 Cycling
Let's Ride: www.letsride.co.uk

Cycling is a great way to get around the Lake District for free, and the Let's Ride site lists dozens of guided rides and bicycle-friendly routes.

2 Bouldering
www.golakes.co.uk

Bouldering, or scrambling, involves climbing rock faces without using specialized equipment. The Lake District tourism website has a directory of companies offering guided tours.

3 Wild Camping
Lake District National Park: www.lakedistrict.gov.uk

With the permission of local landowners it is possible to camp for free in the Lake District. There are strict guidelines you must follow – see the Lake District National Park website.

4 Dark Sky Discovery Sites
Low Gillerthwaite Field Centre: MAP C4; Ennerdale, Cleator; 01946 861229; www.lgfc.org.uk

Dark Sky Discovery Sites are those rare rural locations with minimal light pollution, where on clear nights the Milky Way is stretched between the horizons. Low Gillerthwaite Field Centre in England's most remote valley, Ennerdale, is rated as the country's best site, and free stargazing events are held – weather permitting – throughout the year.

5 Brockhole – the Lake District Visitor Centre

Although you have to pay for parking, Brockhole Visitor Centre boasts several free attractions. For adults, there's a beautiful Arts and Crafts garden by Lake Windermere; there's also an adventure playground for 5–14 year olds and a soft-play area for under-sevens (see p56).

6 Foraging
Galloway Wild Foods: www.gallowaywildfoods.com

There's plenty of foraging to be done in the Lake District, from wild garlic to edible boletus mushrooms and even seaweed, but it's important to know where you can do it and – vitally – what is safe to eat. For information, check the Galloway Wilds Foods website.

Wild campers pitched in an idyllic location overlooking Great Gable

7 Geocaching
Geocaching: www.geo caching.com

If you're not sure how good you are at finding your way around with a map or GPS, geocaching is a fun way to learn, or to test your skills. Sign up on the website and you'll find coordinates for hundreds of secret "caches" hidden away all across the Lake District.

8 Free English Heritage Sites
English Heritage: www.english-heritage.org.uk

A list of free English Heritage historic sites in the Lake District can be found on their website. Among them are Castelrigg Stone Circle, Ambleside Roman Fort, Hardknott Roman Fort and the remains of a Roman bathhouse at Ravenglass *(see p39)*.

Picturesque Holehird Gardens

9 Holehird Gardens
MAP F6 ■ Patterdale Road, Windermere ■ 015394 46008 ■ Open dawn–dusk daily; Visitor information: Apr–Oct: 10am–5pm ■ www.holehird gardens.org.uk

Lovely Holehird Gardens cover 5 ha (12 acres) of hillside, with terraced rockeries and a walled garden. Seasonal displays include alpines, meconopsis poppies and hydrangeas.

10 Audio Self-Guided Walks
Lake District National Park: www.lakedistrict.gov.uk

The Lake District National Park office has three self-guided podcast walks, focusing on Grasmere and Elterwater, exploring how human activity has shaped the region. Each trail is 3–5 km (2–3 miles) long, easy-to-follow and can be downloaded free from the website.

TOP 10 BUDGET TIPS

Getting about by local bus

1 Avoid high parking fees
Parking is limited and expensive throughout the region; hike, cycle or use local buses whenever possible.

2 Visit mid-week
Many hotels and youth hostels drop their prices considerably mid-week, sometimes to half their highest rates.

3 Visit in low season
Though public transport can be limited, visiting outside the peak Easter–September season makes it easier to avoid the crowds.

4 Pack a picnic
Visit a farm shop to stock up on seasonal local produce for a picnic.

5 Save on bus and train tickets
Save money by booking train tickets in advance, and buying Day Ranger passes for local buses *(see pp110–11)*.

6 Use National Trust membership
Members get discounted or free entry to a half-dozen or so National Trust properties around the Lake District.

7 Dine out at lunchtime
Many upmarket restaurants offer fixed-price lunchtime menus and the chance to dine well on a budget.

8 Visit local fairs and events
Enjoy local life at one of the region's many agricultural fairs and shows, mostly held through late summer.

9 Sample a free tastings
Farm shops and breweries often offer free tastings – though you may be expected to buy at the end.

10 Check for discounted tickets
Check online for discounted entry tickets, two-for-one deals or other promotional offers for many of the regional museums and attractions.

Festivals and Events

① Words by the Water
MAP S6 ■ Theatre by the Lake, Keswick ■ www.wayswithwords.co.uk
This ten-day literature festival is held in March. Local author Melvyn Bragg is the Festival President, and the programme is packed with readings and talks by renowned authors.

② Cartmel Races
MAP N4 ■ www.cartmel-racecourse.co.uk
Enjoy a day out at the Cartmel Racecourse in May and July, and on the August bank holiday weekend. There's a huge fairground with food and drink stands and entertainment.

③ Appleby Horse Fair
MAP H3
The little town of Appleby hosts this ancient fair for a week in early June. Begun in 1685, it is still a meeting point for the traveller community; horses are washed in the River Eden, and then traded. Visitors can admire the beautiful painted wooden caravans during this fair.

Wooden caravan at Appleby Horse Fair

④ Derwent Water Regatta
MAP D3 ■ www.nationaltrust.org
Held in early July, the Derwent Water Regatta was revived in 2014 after a 200-year hiatus. A great day of family fun, there are stone-skimming competitions and a bathtub race. You could also try your hand at paddling a kayak, crewing a Viking long ship or just splashing around in the lake.

⑤ Rushbearing
Held in Ambleside in early July and in Grasmere on the closest Saturday to St Oswald's Day (5 Aug), this fascinating archaic ceremony dates back to a time when the earth floor of Cumbrian churches was renewed with rushes. Children carry rush crosses round the village before laying them in the church. They are rewarded with a piece of gingerbread.

⑥ Rydal Sheepdog Trials
MAP F5
For well over a century, the Rydal Sheepdog Trials, held in August, have provided a test of skill for dogs and their handlers. Feisty Swaledale sheep are used, and spectators have a splendid view of the Gathering and the Drive. Fell foxhounds are also shown here, along with working terriers and beagles. There is also a "crooks and sticks" carving competition in which shepherds compete.

⑦ Egremont Crab Fair
MAP B5 ■ www.egremontcrabfair.com
This fair has been held at harvest time almost continuously since 1267. The name refers to the tradition of giving crab apples to fair goers. It also features Cumberland wrestling and gurning (pulling funny faces).

Performance at Summer Music

(8) Lake District Summer Music

www.ldsm.org.uk

Every August, this two-week festival of classical music is held in a range of venues throughout the Lake District. It attracts renowned as well as emerging international musicians.

Cumberland wrestling at Grasmere

(9) Grasmere Sports and Show

MAP E5 ■ www.grasmeresports.com

Held on the Bank Holiday Sunday in August, the Grasmere Vale has been hosting this traditional event since 1868. It includes dog shows, children's races, fell races, Cumberland wrestling and side shows.

(10) World's Biggest Liar

MAP C6 ■ Bridge Inn, Santon Bridge

Locals and a few visitors compete each November to tell the most entertaining tall tale to an exacting pub audience. There are very few rules, but politicians and lawyers are not permitted to join in the fun.

TOP 10 ARTS VENUES

The Old Laundry Theatre

1 Brewery Arts Centre
A creative hub, with cinemas, a theatre and exhibition space (see pp16–17).

2 Theatre by the Lake
A modern theatre in Keswick (see p34).

3 Rosehill Theatre
MAP A4 ■ 01946 692422 ■ Whitehaven
This recently refurbished venue features music, theatre, film, comedy and dance.

4 The Coro
MAP M4 ■ 01229 587140 ■ County Square, Ulverston
The grand Coronation Hall in Ulverston hosts all kinds of art-related events.

5 The Old Laundry Theatre
MAP N2 ■ 015394 40872 ■ Box Office 10am–5pm Mon–Sat ■ Crag Brow, Bowness-on-Windermere
Hosts theatre, music and film events.

6 Zeffirelli's
Zeff's is a restaurant with a cinema and jazz and club nights (see p85).

7 The Kirkgate Centre
MAP C2 ■ 01900 826448 ■ Box office 10am–1pm Mon–Sat
An impressive venue in Cockermouth, offering art house films and theatre.

8 Upfront Puppet Theatre
MAP G2 ■ 017684 84538 ■ Open 10:30am–4:30pm daily ■ Near Hutton in the Forest, Penrith
A fabulous puppet experience in a purpose-built theatre.

9 Alhambra Cinema
This little Art Deco Keswick cinema is a historic gem (see pp34–5).

10 Fellini's
This Mediterranean vegetarian restaurant is also Ambleside's second arthouse cinema (see p85).

Lake District
Area by Area

Rowing boats at Derwent Water

TOP 10 Windermere and the South

Stained glass at Blackwell

The Southern Lakes are very diverse, with the handsome town of Kendal forming the gateway to the area. Beyond Kendal lies Windermere – the name of both the bustling town and the huge lake, dotted with islands and ringed by historic houses such as Blackwell. A little car ferry takes you across the lake to Beatrix Potter's home at Near Sawrey, from where it's a short, waterside drive to picturesque Hawkshead. This is a region of impressive mountains, but one of its lesser-known delights is a series of interesting coastal settlements.

1 Blackwell

One of the most beautiful and best-preserved Arts and Crafts houses in the country, Blackwell was completed in 1900. The vast wood-panelled great hall has a minstrels' gallery, and there is lovely furniture throughout the house, plus well-chosen exhibitions of historical and modern arts and crafts. There is also a fine café *(see p15)*.

Ravenglass steam railway

2 Ravenglass
MAP J2

Set on the estuary of the Esk, Mite and Irt rivers, Ravenglass presents steep façades and high stone walls to the sea. The village with its terraced 19th-century cottages is well worth a look, as are the remains of a Roman bathhouse. It is also home to the steam trains of the Ravenglass and Eskdale Railway *(see p53)*.

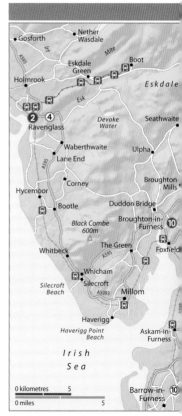

3 Hawkshead
MAP M2

This gem of a village is free from cars, and its cobbled lanes of low, whitewashed cottages are decked out with flowers in summer. Hawkshead's most famous attractions are Wordsworth's

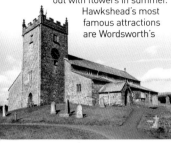

St Michael and All Angels Church

school (see p27) and St Michael and All Angels Church. Beatrix Potter fans should visit the gallery of her work on the main street. The King's Arms is an excellent pub (see p76).

4 Kendal

For a small town, Kendal has some pretty big attractions. There is the Abbot Hall Art Gallery with its fine collection of Romney portraits and contemporary art shows, the evocative Museum of Lakeland Life, the imposing ruins of a 12th-century castle and the buzzing Brewery Arts Centre (see pp16–17). The town's warren of back streets hides some great eating places, including the Waterside Wholefood café (see p77).

AREA MAP OF WINDERMERE AND THE SOUTH

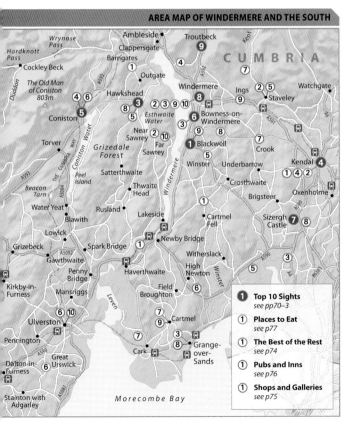

Legend:

1 **Top 10 Sights**
see pp70–3

1 **Places to Eat**
see p77

1 **The Best of the Rest**
see p74

1 **Pubs and Inns**
see p76

1 **Shops and Galleries**
see p75

5 Coniston

MAP M2

An ancient copper-mining village, Coniston has more of a rugged feel to it than the eastern settlements. It sits at the head of the lake, from where you can make a boat trip to Brantwood *(see p31)*, and its old stone cottages offer good accommodation. It also the starting point for walks up the Old Man of Coniston.

BEATRIX POTTER

Potter (1866–1943) came from a wealthy but repressive family. In her thirties she wrote the *Tale of Peter Rabbit*, followed by more than twenty books, bringing her fame and independence. Key to the books' success are their delicate illustrations, and the fact that they are far from saccharine – Mr McGregor did put Peter's dad in a pie and eat him.

Coniston's pretty town centre

6 Bowness-on-Windermere

MAP N2

Bowness sits south of Windermere on the lake shore, and is the jumping off point for boat trips, whether you want a jazz cruise or a jaunt in a canoe. With more of an inviting feel to it than Windermere town itself, Bowness-on-Windermere is a good place for a walk along the shore or to visit the gift shops. Windermere Jetty: Museum of Boats, Steam and Stories *(see pp14–15)* is a big draw for boat enthusiasts as well as kids – it will reopen officially in 2018, but they still run tours for interested visitors: contact them in advance.

7 Sizergh Castle

This fabulous castle was built around a medieval solar tower, the solid core of which is now a rambling and absorbing building. The home of the Strickland family (they go by the name of Hornyold-Strickland) for nearly 800 years, it features an ancestral portrait from 1600, plus a few Romneys as well as glamorous Victorian and Edwardian paintings of the family. Guides offer architectural information and interesting anecdotes about the castle and its inhabitants, and the beautiful grounds include a magnificent limestone rock garden *(see pp16–17)*.

8 Windermere

MAP N2

A Victorian boom town, Windermere attracted rich industrialists by train loads to build grand villas and stone mansions, many of which have now

Boat-trip jetties at Bowness-on-Windermere

been converted into smart B&Bs. While there are no unmissable sights here, it is a good place to stock up for a self-catering trip, and you could also stretch your legs in preparation for tougher fell climbs by walking up to Orrest Head, where you will be rewarded with panoramic views over the lake *(see pp14–15)*.

9 Troutbeck
MAP N1

Just north of Windermere, the village of Troutbeck is the best place to see vernacular Lakes architecture: bulky stone bank barns, porches made of slabs of thin slate and impressive farmhouses with distinctive round chimneys. You can study this style up close at Townend *(see pp14–15)*, a remarkably well-preserved farmhouse with its original furniture still intact. Built in 1626, it was in the same family for over 300 years until it was acquired by the National Trust in the 1940s.

Unspoiled, tranquil Troutbeck

10 Broughton-in-Furness
MAP L3

It is worth a detour from the tourist route to see Broughton-in-Furness, where the huge square of Georgian buildings feels disproportionate for a small country town. The town's wealth derived from its status as a cattle and wool market. Broughton is a good alternative base to the more crowded settlements, with good access for Coniston and Hawkshead to the northeast and the coast and Furness Abbey to the south.

A DRIVE AROUND THE SOUTHERN LAKES

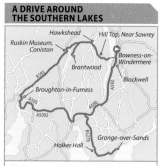

▶ MORNING

From Bowness, take the short drive south to Arts and Crafts **Blackwell** *(see p15)*, an architectural marvel that you cannot miss. Take a break for a morning coffee at the delightful Tea Room here. Afterwards, continue south along the lake on the A592, then head west on the A590. Take a detour to the south (B5278) to see the grandiose gardens of **Holker Hall** *(see p74)*. This is also a good option for lunch, as there is a lovely café here and an excellent food hall, where you can buy all the picnic supplies you'll need. Take your lunch to the promenade at **Grange-over-Sands** *(see p74)* just to the east of Holker Hall.

AFTERNOON

Make your way back on the A590, then take the A5092 and the A595 west to the handsome Georgian market town of **Broughton-in-Furness**. This is well worth a wander. Then travel north on the A593 to Coniston, where you can either visit the **Ruskin Museum** *(see p31)*, or drive round the lake to visit Ruskin's home, **Brantwood** *(see p31)*, though be aware that the house and gardens merit at least an hour. Jumping Jenny *(015394 36373)*, in the former stables of Brantwood, is great for tea. Back in the car, go east through Hawkshead and Near Sawrey, with a stop at Beatrix Potter's home at **Hill Top** *(see p15)*. From here, hop on to a ferry which will take you across the lake and back to Bowness-on-Windermere.

See map on pp70–71

The Best of the Rest

Lakeside & Haverthwaite Railway

 ① Lakeside & Haverthwaite Railway

Kids of all ages will love the short ride on these steam trains *(see p15)*.

② Near Sawrey
MAP M2

This little hamlet's main attraction is Beatrix Potter's beloved farm, Hill Top *(see p15)*, which she bought with the proceeds from her stories.

③ Levens Hall

An ancient tower surrounded by Elizabethan additions, Levens Hall has the oldest topiary gardens in the world, dating from the 1690s *(see p17)*.

 ④ Muncaster Castle
MAP J2 ■ Ravenglass ■ 01229 717614 ■ Castle open: Apr–Oct: noon– 4:30pm Sun–Fri; gardens: Feb–Dec: 10:30am–6pm daily ■ Adm ■ www. muncaster.co.uk

This massive, brooding place is said to be Britain's most haunted castle. The collection of family portraits is outstanding, as are the gardens.

 ⑤ Foulshaw Moss
MAP P3 ■ Off A590 SW of Sizergh ■ 01539 816300 ■ www. cumbriawildlifetrust.org.uk

Between April and August, visitors to this nature reserve have a very good chance of seeing ospreys nesting. It is a short walk to viewing platforms, via boardwalks over extremely boggy ground. Bring binoculars.

 ⑥ Ulverston
MAP M4

Quiet Ulverston is the birthplace of Stan Laurel, and home to the Laurel and Hardy Museum *(see p40)*. It has some great restaurants and shops.

⑦ Holker Hall
MAP M4 ■ Cark-in-Cartmel ■ 01539 558328 ■ Open Apr–Oct: 10:30am–5:30pm Sun–Fri ■ Adm ■ www.holker.co.uk

High Victorian architecture and gardens, complete with a long cascade and statuary.

 ⑧ Grange-over-Sands
MAP N4

This Edwardian resort features a long promenade with palm trees and abundant flowers.

 ⑨ Cartmel
MAP N4

Tiny Cartmel boasts a 12th-century priory *(see p43)* and a two-Michelin-starred restaurant *(see p77)*, plus an excellent village deli selling regional specialities such as sticky toffee pudding and Cumberland sausages.

⑩ Furness Abbey

The ruins of this red sandstone Cistercian abbey, destroyed in the Reformation, provided inspiration to William Wordsworth *(see p42)*.

Romantic ruins of Furness Abbey

Shops and Galleries

1 Museum of Lakeland Life and Industry Gift Shop

This shop offers pottery, local crafts, books on local design and history, traditional toys, cards and historic photographs of Cumbrian shepherds and local festivities *(see p17)*.

2 Booths, Windermere

MAP N2 ▪ Victoria Street, Windermere ▪ 015394 46114

Stock up with supplies for a camping or self-catering trip at this local northwest supermarket chain.

3 Steve Hicks Blacksmiths

MAP N2 ▪ Near Orrest Head, Windermere ▪ 015394 42619

This artisan blacksmith has an attractive workshop with products ranging from candle holders to swirly chairs and benches.

4 Kirkland Books

MAP P2 ▪ Antiques Emporium, Dockray Hall Mill, Kendal ▪ 01539 734849

A family-run business specializing in first editions and signed copies. Titles include works by Alfred Wainwright and Beatrix Potter.

5 Hawkshead Relish Company

MAP M2 ▪ The Square, Hawkshead ▪ 015394 36614 ▪ www.hawkshead relish.com

A lip-smacking selection of relishes, chutneys and jams are sold here in a historic building in Hawkshead, as well as being available throughout the Lake District.

6 Yew Tree Barn

MAP N4 ▪ Low Newton ▪ 015395 31498 ▪ www.yewtree barn.co.uk

Antiques, gifts and bric-a-brac cram this stone-built barn. There is a section for reclaimed pieces including fire-places, baths and artists' studios. Make time for a coffee in Harry's Café Bar.

7 Kentmere Pottery

MAP P1 ▪ Kentmere, near Kendal ▪ 01539 821621 ▪ Open Mon–Fri (times vary; call for details)

Gordon Fox sells his own ceramics, including the exquisite Snowdrop Collection, from his studio by an ancient mill. Gordon specializes in lamps, tableware and decorated boxes, as well as taking on special commissions for clients.

Low Sizergh Barn's farm shop

8 Low Sizergh Barn

This beautiful 18th-century barn sells local food – including their own produce – as well as clothes, homeware, handmade paper, pottery, rugs and a range of natural skincare products *(see pp16–17)*.

9 Blackwell Shop

This shop has a good range of contemporary pottery, with vases, tiles, crockery and bowls. They also stock a selection of books on crafts and architecture *(see p15)*.

10 Two by Two

MAP M4 ▪ 52 Market Street, Ulverston ▪ 01229 480703 ▪ www. twobytwoonline.com

This boutique sells bright scarves and clothes made from natural fibres. There is also a great book-shop, Sutton's, nearby *(see p62)*.

See map on pp70–71

Pubs and Inns

(1) The Masons Arms
MAP N3 ■ Strawberry Bank, Cartmel Fell ■ 015395 68486

Stop off at the Masons Arms for fine ales, a friendly welcome, excellent food and views of the Winster Valley.

(2) Eagle & Child Inn
MAP P2 ■ Staveley
■ 01539 821320

An archetypal village inn on the river Kent in Staveley, the Eagle & Child has a lovely garden. Combine with a visit to the craft outlets at Mill Yard in the village.

(3) Hole in t'Wall
MAP N2 ■ Lowside, Bowness
■ 015394 43488

This atmospheric early 17th-century inn in Bowness is a short walk from Windermere. Sit outside on the stone terrace or head for the cosy, beamed and wood-panelled interior.

(4) The Sun
MAP M2 ■ Coniston
■ 015394 41248

A Coniston classic, handily located at the base of the path to the Old Man of Coniston (see p30). The Sun has a spacious terrace, and the bar serves eight local ales on handpump.

(5) Hawkshead Brewery Beer Hall
MAP P2 ■ Mill Yard, Staveley ■ 01539 825260

Next door to legendary Wilf's Café, this stone-built beer hall is a great location to try the beers brewed on site.

Beers on tap at Hawkshead Brewery

Picturesque Black Bull pub

(6) Black Bull
MAP M2 ■ Yewdale Road, Coniston ■ 015394 41335

The whitewashed Black Bull brews its own bitters and ales: it is the perfect refuge for a post-walk pint.

(7) Sun Inn
MAP N2 ■ Crook
■ 01539 821351

A traditional and largely unchanged village inn, converted from mill workers' cottages. Although off the beaten track, it draws lots of visitors.

(8) Kings Arms
A 500-year-old inn in the heart of Hawkshead, the Kings Arms offers decent bar meals, real ales and an impressive selection of malt whiskies. The beer garden is idyllic in the summertime (see p117).

(9) Watermill Inn & Brewery
MAP N2 ■ Ings, near Windermere
■ 01539 821309

This award-winning pub with its own microbrewery is popular with beer aficionados and all those that enjoy a cosy, welcoming atmosphere.

(10) Cuckoo Brow Inn
MAP M2 ■ Far Sawrey
■ 015394 43425

A great place to stay or eat and a good base for visiting key Lakeland tourist destinations such as Beatrix Potter's Hill Top Farm, which is within easy walking distance.

Places to Eat

PRICE CATEGORIES

For a three-course meal for one with half a bottle of wine (or equivalent meal), taxes and extra charges.

£ under £35   ££ £35–50   £££ over £50

1 Drunken Duck
MAP N1 ▪ Barngates, Ambleside ▪ 015394 36347 ▪ £££

The best of British food is served in this country pub, which has an upmarket feel. Mains include Herdwick lamb shoulder and ox cheek; there are also plenty of vegetarian options (see p117).

2 Waterside Wholefood
MAP P2 ▪ Kent View, Kendal ▪ 01539 729743 ▪ Closed Sun ▪ £

This terrific vegetarian café with a whitewashed interior and chunky wooden furniture is in a lovely setting on a footpath by the river in the heart of Kendal. Dishes are hearty.

3 The Hazelmere
MAP N4 ▪ Yewbarrow Terrace, Grange-over-Sands ▪ 01539 532972 ▪ £

A stylish café serving light meals, such as local potted shrimps, as well as very possibly the best afternoon teas in the entire Lake District.

4 Holbeck Ghyll Country House Hotel
MAP N2 ▪ Holbeck Lane, Windermere ▪ 015394 32375 ▪ £££

A contender for the best restaurant in the Lake District, serving delicious locally sourced food in a beautiful setting with breathtaking views of the Langdale Pikes (see p116).

5 The Brown Horse Inn
MAP N2 ▪ Sunny Bank Road, Winster, Windermere ▪ 015394 43443 ▪ £

Terrific and tasty pub food and beer from its own micro-brewery. Book ahead for dinner at weekends, as this place is very popular (see p117).

6 The General Burgoyne
MAP L5 ▪ Great Urswick, near Ulverston ▪ 01229 586394 ▪ Closed Mon ▪ ££

This looks like a simple pub from the outside, but the food is spectacular.

7 L'Enclume
MAP N4 ▪ Cavendish Street, Cartmel ▪ 015395 36362 ▪ £££

Two-Michelin-starred L'Enclume serves delicate, delicious food using home-grown and foraged produce.

8 Hrishi, Gilpin Hotel & Lake House
MAP N2 ▪ Crook Road, Windermere ▪ 015394 88818 ▪ £££

Sumptuous dining and wonderful service in one of the most elegant hotels in the Lakes (see p116).

9 The Samling
MAP N2 ▪ Ambleside Road, Windermere ▪ 01539 431922 ▪ ££

This Michelin-starred restaurant offers some of the finest dining in the Lakes. A kitchen garden provides in-season vegetables, and the chef loves to experiment (see p116).

The Samling's inventive cuisine

10 Miller Howe
MAP N2 ▪ Rayrigg Road, Windermere ▪ 01539 442536 ▪ £££

Superbly cooked and well-presented dishes that use locally reared meat are served here. Miller Howe also offers exquisite puddings.

See map on pp70–71

TOP 10 The Central Fells

This is perhaps the most enchanting part of the Lake District, cut through by magnificent Langdale, where undulating stone walls climb the fells, giving way to steeper peaks. At the valley bottom rushes the river Brathay, edged with paths for walkers. The area is blessed with two lovely settlements: Ambleside, with its excellent restaurant scene, and Grasmere, forever linked with Wordsworth. March is a classic time to visit to see the daffodils in full bloom – but be aware that snowstorms are still a distinct possibility then.

Elegant interior of Rydal Mount

1 Rydal Mount

This was Wordsworth's home for the last 37 years of his life and it is quite a contrast with the cramped conditions of Dove Cottage. In the library at Rydal Mount you can see the couch upon which the poet lay, and there is a good collection of paintings, letters and ephemera, including Wordsworth's lunch box and his sister Dorothy's tiny shoes. There's also a tea room (see pp26–7).

2 Grasmere

There is a good reason why Grasmere gets overrun with visitors: it is probably the prettiest village in the Lakes, and is backed by some of the most magnificent fells. It is rich in Wordsworthian associations: he is buried in St Oswald's graveyard – the interior of the church is worth a look for its impressive beamed roof, too. There are also plenty of cafés, a decent village pub, great accommodation and terrific walks (see pp12–13).

3 Great Langdale
MAP E5
Great Langdale offers the scenery of the Lake District on a grand scale: it is studded with stands of mature

AREA MAP OF THE CENTRAL FELLS

1	**Top 10 Sights** see pp78–81
1	**Places to Eat** see p85
1	**Pubs and Inns** see p84
1	**Shops and Galleries** see p83
1	**Beauty Spots** see p82

Stickle Tarn

The Cumbria Way

Browney Gill

Blea Tarn

Mosdale

Wrynose Pass

Cockley Beck

Hardknott Pass

Tranquil waters of Grasmere

Great Langdale, ringed by magnificent peaks and crags

trees, and the meadows are scattered with wild flowers in summer. Around the valley rise iconic mountains such as Bowfell, Crinkle Crags and the Langdale Pikes, landmarks in themselves, and in the history of climbing in this area. Their peaks are often shrouded by low clouds, and these mountains have an imposing, sometimes formidable aspect. However, this is what makes them irresistible to the large numbers of walkers and climbers who come here.

④ Dove Cottage

Wordsworth's home from 1799 to 1808 is a richly evocative place, at once charming and plain. The family lived an austere life here – Walter Scott reported that they ate three meals a day, two of which were porridge. Knowledgeable guides bring the cottage to life, while the adjoining museum has some fascinating memorabilia – you can see William's court suit, panama hat and toothscrapers (see pp26–7).

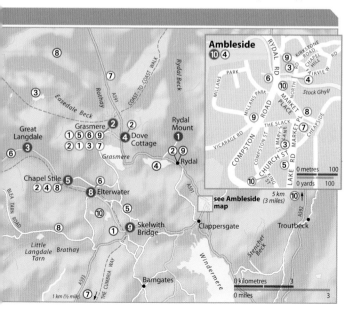

Former quarry village of Chapel Stile

SLATE MINING

Above Chapel Stile, the scars of the slate mine are very visible – you can take a footpath to the Elterwater quarry and peer over the edge at the valley of raw green slate. It's still a working mine, though on a much reduced scale from its 19th-century heyday, when a nearby gunpowder works supplied the mine, and the workers cottages were built.

5 Chapel Stile
MAP E5

This little quarry settlement is the next village up the valley from Elterwater, but it has more of a rugged feel, with its terraces of quarrymen's cottages and with the scars of the massive slate quarry visible above. The eponymous chapel is plain but attractive – have a look inside at the modern tapestry relating the history of the village. Brambles café (see p85) above the Co-op is a fine place for a coffee, while Wainwrights' Inn (see p84) on the edge of Chapel Stile is an essential stop for walkers.

6 Hardknott Pass
MAP D6

You need to brace yourself for the steep zigzag drive over the Hardknott Pass – it is definitely not an attractive option for fearful drivers. However, the views go from impressive to jaw-dropping as you gain in elevation, and the remains of the Roman fort are unmissable, comprising long snaking lines of stone walls. The fort was built during Hadrian's reign, and contained a bath house amongst other buildings, though creature comforts are hard to imagine at this wild, windswept spot.

7 The Cumbria Way
MAP E5 ■ www.ldwa.org.uk

This long-distance path crosses stunning countryside in the Central Fells, on the 113-km (70-mile) route between Ulverston in the south and Carlisle in the north. It's a great way to explore Coniston and Langdale. The flat stretch along the river between Elterwater and Chapel Stile is particularly attractive, and provides some gorgeous views.

8 Elterwater
MAP E5

This pretty little village sits on the river, and enjoys a wonderful aspect below the high fells. There's not much in the way of sights, but it's an ideal, tranquil base for walkers and cyclists. In summer you can take a seat outside the Britannia Inn, and you'll be sure to fall into conversation with fellow walkers. Coniston and Grasmere are also good destinations for hikes from the village.

Ambleside's charming centre

9 Skelwith Bridge
MAP E6

Skelwith Bridge sits at the end of Langdale and is the starting point for many walks. It is a tiny, pretty place that clusters around the bridge over the Brathay – Chesters by the River *(see p25)* is a popular upmarket eating place, and you can buy items made from the distinctive local green slate in the adjoining shop. A stroll upriver takes you to Skelwith Force *(see p82)*.

Skelwith Bridge, over the Brathay

10 Ambleside
The town of Ambleside has an enjoyably sophisticated atmosphere, plus lively cafés and upmarket restaurants. The Armitt Museum showcases the work of Kurt Schwitters *(see p54)*, the émigré artist who lived here after the war, and watercolours by Beatrix Potter. There is a fine short walk from the heart of the village up the ghyll, and it is also a good base for excursions in Langdale *(see pp20–21)*.

A WORDSWORTHIAN WALK IN THE CENTRAL FELLS

Grasmere
Dove Cottage
Coffin Trail
Rydal Mount
Rydal Hall
Faeryland
Grasmere Lake
Rydal Water
Dora's Field

▶ MORNING

Your starting point is **Grasmere** *(see p78)*, where the plain graves of Wordsworth, his wife, sister and children can be seen in the graveyard of **St Oswald's Church**. Wander on to **Dove Cottage** *(see p79)*, located just east of the village near the main road, where the cottage tour and a visit to the museum will take at least an hour. From here, head up the lane and follow signs for the **Coffin Trail** *(see p12)*, used to carry corpses from Rydal to their resting place in St Oswald's (look out for the stone coffin rests along the way). The walk leads you parallel to the road, but high above it, away from the traffic.

AFTERNOON

After around an hour you reach Rydal, where the riverside tea-shop in the grounds of **Rydal Hall** *(see p82)* is a decent spot for lunch. Backtrack slightly to visit Rydal Mount *(see p78)*, the poet's home for the last 37 years of his life. Then head down the hill to the church – through the church-yard you reach **Dora's Field** *(see p82)*, planted with daffodils by the Wordsworths when their much loved daughter died. From here, cross over the road, turn right for a few metres and leave the road to cross the little bridge. A path leads you along **Rydal Water**, and then to the foot of Grasmere lake *(see p78)*. You join a lane for the final stretch that circles back to Grasmere village. On the way back into the village, drop in at the charming outdoor tea room of **Faeryland** *(see p12)* on the lake for refreshments (summer only).

See map on pp78–9 ◀

Beauty Spots

 1 Skelwith Force
MAP E6

This force (waterfall) lies just west of Skelwith Bridge on the riverside path. Continue past the waterfall to reach the Cumbria Way route, which winds along the river to Elterwater.

2 Dora's Field

The field below Rydal Mount was planted up with daffodils by Wordsworth and his wife after the death of their daughter Dora. March is the best time to visit if you wish to see the flowers in bloom (see p26).

3 Easedale Tarn
MAP E5

A stiff but wonderful hike from Grasmere leads to Easedale Tarn – one of Wordsworth's favourite spots.

4 Rydal Water
MAP F5

A scenic path runs west along Rydal Water, connecting Rydal with Grasmere, via the attractive little outdoor tea room and boat rental outfit at Faeryland.

5 Loughrigg Tarn
MAP E5

This lovely little body of water sits north of Skelwith Bridge and at the base of Loughrigg Fell. The views from the top of the Fell are considered to be some of the best in the lakes.

Loughrigg Tarn from the Fell

6 Stickle Ghyll
MAP E5

A very steep and rough path from the New Dungeon Ghyll Hotel takes you past the waterfalls and rock pools of rushing Stickle Ghyll to the high tarn.

 7 Tarn Hows

This beautiful site is an ideal place for families to enjoy walking around the tarn. An early morning or evening visit is recommended to appreciate the stunning views.

 8 Helm Crag
MAP E5

The peaks of Helm Crag are called the Howitzer, and The Lion and the Lamb (referring to the distinctive shape of this group of rocks). Alfred Wainwright called the Howitzer "a brief essay in real mountaineering".

 9 Rydal Hall
MAP F5

Rydal Hall, opposite Rydal Mount, is a stately Neo-Classical home owned by the diocese of Carlisle. The sweeping grounds are home to the Full Circle campsite (see p119).

10 Elterwater
MAP E5

This is a gleaming lake fed by the Brathay, just below the village of Elterwater. Take the path round the lake and on to Ambleside. There is also a bus back to Elterwater.

Shops and Galleries

Sarah Nelson's Gingerbread Shop

1 Sarah Nelson's Gingerbread Shop

Local gingerbread is one of the characteristic tastes and fragrant smells of Grasmere. Baked in the village according to a secret recipe, developed in 1854 by resourceful cook Sarah Nelson, the gingerbread is sold in this little shop next to St Oswald's Church (see p13).

2 The Shop at Dove Cottage

Everything you have ever wanted to know about the Romantic poets can be found here. There is a full range of poetry titles and biographies, CDs and DVDs, plus notebooks, soaps and other gifts (see pp12–13).

3 Below Stairs

MAP F5 ■ Church Street, Ambleside ■ 015394 34370 ■ www.below-stairs.co.uk

This is a wonderful shop in which to browse for china, kitchen gadgets, place mats, pepper mills and all sorts of hard-to-find kitchenware.

4 Outdoor Shops

MAP F5 ■ Ambleside

Ambleside has more outdoor shops than you can believe, so it is a good place to visit if you need to add to your hiking, climbing and mountain-biking kit. You can also pick up local maps and guidebooks here.

5 Sam Read's Bookshop

A well-informed owner and a characterful space distinguish this little bookshop, founded in 1887, in the heart of Grasmere. Its shelves are stacked with local-interest titles, guidebooks and contemporary fiction, plus there's a strong children's section (see p13).

6 Heaton Cooper Studio

This is an elegant family-run studio and gallery that deals in paintings and prints – often of the surrounding area – as well as sculpture, pottery and a fabulous range of art materials (see p13).

7 Old Courthouse Gallery

MAP F5 ■ Market Place, Ambleside ■ 015394 32022

The Old Courthouse Gallery is one of the largest independent contemporary art galleries in the Lakes, featuring local paintings, crafts, quirky furniture, clocks and handmade glass pieces.

8 Langdale Co-Operative

MAP E5 ■ Chapel Stile ■ 015394 33124

Founded in the 19th century, this village Co-op is a good place for campers and self-caterers (who can order in advance, for collection) to stock up. There is also a café.

9 Lakeland Art Gallery

MAP E5 ■ Grasmere ■ 015394 35271

Around for over 30 years, this gallery offers paintings and signed limited-edition prints. It specializes in scenes from around the Lake District.

10 Fred's Ambleside Bookshop

MAP F5 ■ Ambleside ■ 015394 33388

This quaint little store located near the Salutation Hotel in Ambleside is great for maps and guidebooks, as well as fiction and history titles, many of which have a local connection.

See map on pp78–9

Pubs and Inns

Visitors and locals enjoying the sunshine outside The Britannia Inn

① Sticklebarn
MAP E5 ■ Great Langdale
■ 015394 37356

This cosy pub sits at the very foot of the fells, and serves simple but tasty bar meals with a selection of real ales.

② 1769 Bar and Restaurant
MAP E5 ■ Grasmere ■ 015394 35456

Part of the Inn at Grasmere, this lively pub is the locals' choice, with a good selection of beers. There is a limited menu of bar meals.

③ The Unicorn
MAP F5 ■ North Road, Ambleside ■ 015394 33216

Tucked away in a steep part of the village, this is a welcoming, old-fashioned pub with live music and a good range of whiskies.

④ Wainwrights' Inn
MAP E5 ■ Chapel Stile
■ 015394 38088

This walker's favourite, in a lovely location just outside Chapel Stile, serves hearty portions of local food, such as Cumberland sausages.

⑤ Old Dungeon Ghyll Hotel
A venerable Lakes inn that features the excellent and rugged Hikers' Bar, There is an outdoor terrace, perfect for a summer pint. The twelve bedrooms are furnished in comfy country style (see p119).

⑥ The Britannia Inn
This inn sits in one of the most picturesque pub locations in the Lakes, on Elterwater's village green, and is packed with walkers and locals on summer evenings. The en-suite rooms are very comfortable (see p118).

⑦ The Traveller's Rest
An ancient inn, sitting on the road north from Grasmere, with cosy rooms for those who want to stay over. It is a good spot for avoiding the crowds in the village (see p119).

⑧ Three Shires Inn
MAP E6 ■ Little Langdale
■ 015394 37215

This remote inn is a popular stop for walkers in Langdale, and a jumping off point for some great hikes.

⑨ Golden Rule
MAP F5 ■ Smithy Brow
■ 015394 32257

A traditional pub in Ambleside with a fine selection of real ales, a patio garden and strictly no music – it is very popular with locals and walkers.

⑩ Kirkstone Pass Inn
MAP F5 ■ Kirkstone Pass
■ 015394 33888

This 500-year-old pub sits in a truly remote, sometimes cloud-fringed location on the high Kirkstone Pass (see p52). It has low ceilings, flagstone floors and a timber-framed interior.

Places to Eat

PRICE CATEGORIES

For a three-course meal for one with half a bottle of wine (or equivalent meal), taxes and extra charges.

£ under £35   ££ £35–50   £££ over £50

1 Miller Howe Café
MAP E5 ■ Grasmere ■ 015394 35234 ■ £

This friendly café is the best option for a full English breakfast in Grasmere. It also offers delicious cakes and scones, plus good coffee.

2 Brambles
MAP E5 ■ Chapel Stile ■ 015394 37500 ■ £

On the top floor of the historic Langdale Co-op, Brambles is an attractive and friendly little village café, with a wooden interior, good coffee and excellent pastries.

Jumble Room's arty interior

3 Jumble Room
MAP E5 ■ Langdale Road, Grasmere ■ 015394 35188 ■ ££

Jumble Room's international menu includes Italian and Catalan dishes. Closer to home, the beer-battered fish and chips is also very popular.

4 Rattle Gill Café
MAP F5 ■ Ambleside ■ 015394 31321 ■ £

This cute and friendly café is one of a cluster of attractive white-painted buildings opposite the waterwheel.

5 Old Stamp House
MAP F5 ■ Church Street, Ambleside ■ 015394 32775 ■ £££

This is fine dining at its very best in Ambleside, but in a relaxed, unstuffy atmosphere. Local ingredients are put to good use to create a small but superb menu that will please vegetarians and meat-eaters alike. Open for lunch and dinner.

6 The Apple Pie
MAP F5 ■ Rydal Road, Ambleside ■ 015394 33679 ■ £

This bustling café serves a great apple pie, as its name suggests, as well as other delicious sweet and savoury baked goods. Walkers (and their dogs) are always welcome.

7 Green's
MAP E5 ■ College Street, Grasmere ■ 015394 35790 ■ £

Green's delicious menu offers local and seasonal food, as well as a selection of gluten- and dairy-free, vegan and vegetarian dishes

8 Doi Intanon
MAP F5 ■ Market Place, Ambleside ■ 015394 32119 ■ £

If you are starting to grow tired of Cumberland sausage, try some flavourful Thai food at this attractive restaurant in central Ambleside.

9 Zeffirelli's
MAP F5 ■ Compston Road, Ambleside ■ 015394 33845 ■ £

One of Ambleside's hotspots, Zeffirelli's serves delicious vege-tarian mains, pizzas and very large puddings. There is a jazz club upstairs, and a great cinema too.

10 Fellini's
MAP F5 ■ Church Street, Ambleside ■ 015394 32487 ■ ££

A sister restaurant of Zeffirelli's, the stylish Fellini's also serves vegetarian food and has its own cinema screen, although it is a more upmarket venue.

See map on pp78–9

TOP 10 Ullswater

Tucked into the northeast of the region, glacial Ullswater is a wonderfully scenic destination, geared up for tourists without being overrun by them. One of the highlights is a pleasurable ride on the historic steamboat, taking you from Glenridding in the south via Howtown to attractive Pooley Bridge in the northeast. This area is renowned for its majestic scenery. Glenridding is the starting point for hikes up Helvellyn, while a less ambitious walk takes you to the gushing falls of Aira Force.

One of the Dacre Bears

1 Ullswater Steamer

MAP F4 ■ Glenridding
■ 017684 82229 ■ Runs daily ■ Adm
■ www.ullswater-steamers.co.uk

Long and elegant, the red-funnelled converted Victorian steamers are a fine sight on Ullswater, ferrying passengers up and down the lake from Glenridding to Pooley Bridge, with a stop halfway at Howtown. Special-interest cruises include bird- and wildlife-watching trips and photography cruises.

Victorian Ullswater Steamer

AREA MAP OF ULLSWATER

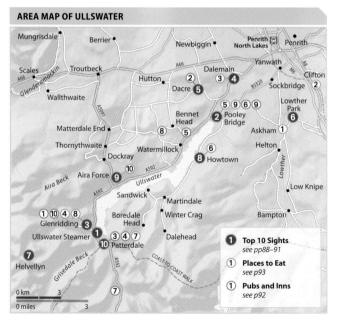

	Top 10 Sights see pp88–91
1	**Places to Eat** see p93
1	**Pubs and Inns** see p92

Previous pages Valley south of Keswick with a view towards Buttermere

2 Pooley Bridge
MAP G3

Despite its namesake high-arched stone-built bridge over the river Eamont being totally destroyed during the terrible floods of 2015, Pooley Bridge remains a handsome lakeside village, and a lovely spot for waterside picnics. It can be busy in summer, as it is a stop on the steamer route, though several good walks start nearby. Head on to nearby Moor Divock to visit Bronze Age remains, including The Cockpit a well-preserved circle of 75 stones. The best pub in the village is the 18th-century Sun Inn, which sits near the main square *(see p92)*.

3 Glenridding
MAP F4

Extending from the shores of Ullswater up the steep sides of the fells, Glenridding is a pleasing little village. There are no great sights but that is compensated for by a lively holiday atmosphere. Some old-fashioned village shops, outdoor stores and a few cafés and pubs are sustained by the hordes of walkers who come here in all weathers to tackle nearby Helvellyn. Outdoor types will head up to the remote Helvellyn hostel, or pitch up at the idyllic Gillside campsite. There are many easier treks for less intrepid walkers.

Glenridding, overlooking Ullswater

Dalemain's handsome stairwell

4 Dalemain
MAP G3 ▪ 017684 86450
▪ **Open Apr–Oct: 10:30am–3:30pm Sun–Thu** ▪ **Adm** ▪ **www.dalemain.com**

Like many Lake District houses, Dalemain has been in the same family for a very long time – more than 300 years in this case. An elegant pink-hued Georgian façade conceals the building's real age: it was built around a 12th-century defensive tower and is mainly Elizabethan. In addition to the panelled interiors and family portraits, there is a good café in the medieval hall. The children's garden has a lovely sleeping giant sculpture.

THE VIKINGS IN ULLSWATER

There is evidence for Viking settlement at Ullswater in the very name of the lake – it is thought to have been called after a chieftain, Ulf, who ruled the area 1,200 years ago. An alternative suggestion is that it was named in honour of the Viking God Ullr. The earthworks on the northeastern shoreline are reputed to conceal the remains of a fortified Viking settlement.

Winter trekking on Helvellyn

Dacre
MAP G3

Attractive Dacre village is home to romantic 14th-century Dacre Castle. Nearby is a restored Norman church, St Andrew's: fragments of Viking crosses can be seen in the chancel, and in the graveyard sit four stone effigies, known as the Dacre Bears. The charming Horse & Farrier pub (see p92), completes the picture.

6 Lowther Park
MAP G3 ▪ Bird of Prey Centre; 01931 712746; open Apr–Oct: 11am–5pm daily; flying demonstrations: 2–4pm ▪ Adm

This is the estate of an imposing Victorian-Gothic castle, whose impressive ruin lends the park an air of melancholy. Two of the villages on the estate are lined with painted Georgian houses, and there is a children's play area Bird of Prey Centre, where you can watch kestrels and falcons in action. A farm building here has been converted into a very pleasant teashop.

7 Helvellyn
MAP E4

The third-highest mountain in England, Helvellyn is quite popular. The narrow Striding Edge ascent is as edgy as it sounds, and involves a scramble to the summit. There are plenty of other less perilous ways of tackling it, but, whichever route you go for, do not ascend Helvellyn unless you are well equipped and reasonably fit. Detailed and current advice on routes and weather conditions can be obtained at the tourist information centre at Glenridding.

8 Howtown
MAP G4

The Ullswater Steamer drops many walkers at Howtown, which is little more than a row of houses and the Howtown Hotel. Above the village, follow the road uphill to the lovely St Martin's, a plain Elizabethan church

Lowther Park's ruined castle

embraced by a yew tree. To walk to Patterdale, follow the lakeshore route or head through the Boredale valley, with a dramatic ascent and descent at the end of the walk.

(9) Aira Force
MAP F4

There are a large number of walks to waterfalls in the Lakes, but this is one of the most satisfying. Aira Force, 20 m (66 ft), is framed by two stone bridges. William and Dorothy Wordsworth visited the surrounding hills in 1802, and it was her diary entry describing the daffodils that prompted one of the most famous poems in the English language. The footpaths continue beyond the waterfall to Dockray.

View over Patterdale

(10) Patterdale
MAP F4

Patterdale (named for St Patrick) is another pleasant and low-key little settlement that sits in a cluster on the road to Glenridding. The village is a starting point for a number of walks. There are a couple of pubs here, notably the walkers' favourite the White Lion, plus a good chalet-style youth hostel, and a waterside campsite: Side Farm. This is worth a visit for non-campers too, as there is an excellent little teashop in the farmyard, which is located beside an 18th-century barn *(see p93)*.

A DAY IN ULLSWATER

Pooley Bridge

Dockray

Aira Force Tearoom, Aira Force

Howtown

Glenridding

St Martin's Church

Patterdale

▶ MORNING

Starting from **Glenridding** *(see p89)*, take the bus along the western side of the lake (this is not a particularly pleasant walk due to traffic on the lake road). After a couple of miles, get off the bus for the signposted walk up to **Aira Force**. This walk takes around 40 minutes there and back, although the path continues uphill to the village of Dockray, if you want to carry on. You can have morning coffee at the charming little **Aira Force Tearooms** *(see p93)* at the start of the walk. Get back on the bus, and carry on up the northern shore to **Pooley Bridge** *(see p89)*, where you can relax over lunch at the **Sun Inn** or the **Pooley Bridge Inn** *(see p92)*.

AFTERNOON

From Pooley Bridge, take the historic steamer down the lake. You could return directly to Glenridding, or disembark at **Howtown**. From here, follow the lane uphill to **St Martin's Church**. Either retrace your steps to the ferry or – if you have the time, energy and an OS map – follow the track and footpath for the wonderful hike to **Patterdale** before making your way back to Glenridding. You have a choice of two very distinct walking routes – the low-level option takes you along the lakeshore to Patterdale, whereas the route through Boredale involves a steep climb to ascend the valley wall, from where you dip down into the village – a gorgeous sight in the early evening light.

See map on p88

Pubs and Inns

① Traveller's Rest
MAP F4 ■ Glenridding
■ 017684 82298

Head up the hill in the village to reach this ancient inn, the best in the area. There is a terrace for the summer months, and it is often packed with walkers.

② Horse & Farrier
MAP G3 ■ Dacre ■ 017684 86541

Tucked away in one of the quietest and prettiest villages in the Ullswater area, this venerable 18th-century pub makes a perfect stop for a pint. The outdoor seating and the wholesome food are a bonus for walkers.

③ White Lion
MAP F4 ■ Patterdale ■ 017684 82214

Good food and real ales are served in this classic and convivial village inn. The food, which is above-average pub grub, really hits the spot if you have been on a long walk.

④ Patterdale Hotel
MAP F4 ■ Patterdale ■ 017684 82231

The hotel's Place Fell Inn is nice for an alfresco drink; the beer garden is a lush spot to relax in the summer sun with a pint of good local ale.

⑤ Brackenrigg Inn
MAP G3 ■ Ullswater ■ 017684 86206

This traditional wayside inn on the northern shore of the lake has a basic Wi-Fi enabled bar, as well as a more upmarket dining room and lovely views from the terrace.

⑥ Pooley Bridge Inn
MAP G3 ■ Pooley Bridge
■ 017684 86215

An unusual balconied building, this inn is in the centre of Pooley Bridge. It is wreathed with hanging baskets in summer; inside, there is a timber ceiling and log fires when it is cold.

⑦ Brotherswater Inn
MAP F5 ■ Brotherswater
■ 017684 82239

This wayside inn is situated near the Kirkstone Pass, on the road to Ullswater. It is very popular with ale-drinking hikers (see p118).

The Quiet Bar's characterful interior

⑧ The Quiet Bar
MAP F3 ■ Quiet Site Holiday Park, Ullswater ■ 07768 727016

This quirky campsite bar was converted from an ancient barn in the 1950s. It is worth spending a night in a pod or Hobbit Hole to sample the "Quiet Pint" – the site's own brew.

⑨ Sun Inn
MAP G3 ■ Pooley Bridge
■ 017684 82444

Housed in a whitewashed building, which was converted from a row of ancient cottages, the Sun Inn serves Jennings Ales, including the bizarrely named Cock-a-Hoop bitter and Sneck-Lifter ale.

⑩ The Ramblers Bar
MAP F4 ■ Inn on the Lake, Glenridding ■ 017684 82444

The bar is located in an annexe to the Inn on the Lake hotel, prettily placed on the Ullswater shore. There is real ale, large pub meals and snooker.

See map on p88

Places to Eat

1 Queen's Head Inn
MAP G3 ■ Lower Green, Askham ■ 01931 712225 ■ £
This friendly pub, with two open fires, lies on the eastern edge of the National Park. It offers a substantial menu of hearty fare and a selection of tapas.

2 George and Dragon
MAP H3 ■ Clifton, near Penrith
■ 01768 865381 ■ ££
Much of the produce at this restored coaching inn is sourced from the Lowther Park Estate *(see p90)*.

3 Dalemain Tearoom
MAP G3 ■ Dalemain House
■ 017684 86450 ■ Open Apr–Dec ■ £
Try the tea and cakes or a light lunch in a medieval hall, part of Dalemain's wonderful mix of historic buildings.

4 Inn on the Lake
MAP F4 ■ Glenridding
■ 017684 82444 ■ ££
This lakeside hotel is a convenient stop for afternoon tea or dinner; you can enjoy the view across the lake from the terrace or lounge while tucking into the tasty traditional fare made from local produce.

Beautifully sited Inn on the Lake

5 Treetops
MAP G3 ■ Pooley Bridge
■ 017684 86267 ■ £
This is a reliable stop for coffee or a light lunch in the centre of Pooley Bridge. There are a few outdoor seats.

6 Sharrow Bay Hotel
MAP G4 ■ 017684 86301 ■ £££
This plush hotel on the eastern side of the lake offers a bird's-eye view of the water lapping below as you enjoy high tea, good-value lunch or the fine-dining, 10-course tasting menu.

7 Side Farm Tearoom
MAP F4 ■ Side Farm Camping, near Patterdale ■ 077961 28897 ■ £
Home baking, hot drinks and ice creams are served in the summer in this lovely little tearoom.

8 Fellbites
MAP F4 ■ Glenridding
■ 017684 82781 ■ £
Set in a handsome ochre-coloured house, Fellbites serves hearty, reasonably priced dishes. The little patch of garden is a good suntrap.

9 Granny Dowbekin's
MAP G3 ■ Pooley Bridge
■ 017684 86453 ■ £
The garden at Granny Dowbekin's offers the best view of Pooley Bridge. The tearoom specializes in all-day breakfasts and features fresh bakes.

10 Aira Force Tearooms
MAP F4 ■ At the foot of Aira Force ■ 017684 82067 ■ £
Good for a pre- or post-walk cup of tea, a hearty soup or sandwiches.

TOP 10 The Northwest

The northwest of the region has plenty of contrasts – Borrowdale is one of the most verdant valleys in the Lakes, with lofty mountains and enticing hamlets, while at Honister the landscape is at its starkest and most forbidding. There is a welcoming stately home at Mirehouse, on the shores of Bassenthwaite Lake, while to the west are deprived coastal towns such as Workington. The busy tourist town of Keswick sits on the shores of Derwent Water with mighty Skiddaw looming over it. Just outside the national park sits Cockermouth, a handsome Georgian settlement most famous for the National Trust property Wordsworth House.

Keswick rowing boat

AREA MAP OF THE NORTHWEST

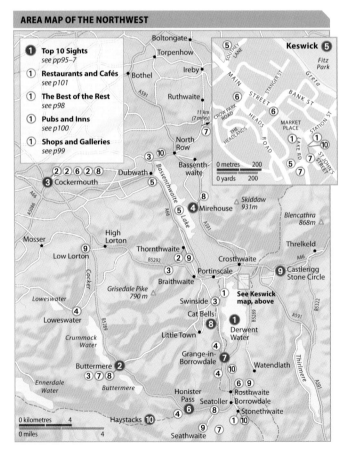

	Top 10 Sights see pp95–7
①	Restaurants and Cafés see p101
①	The Best of the Rest see p98
①	Pubs and Inns see p100
①	Shops and Galleries see p99

Keswick 5

The spectacular lake of Derwent Water viewed from on high

 Derwent Water
MAP D3 ▪ Derwent Water Marina: 017687 72912; www.derwentwatermarina.co.uk

Derwent Water is one of the loveliest of the Lakes, and one of the easiest to explore by boat. The Keswick Launch makes regular circuits from Keswick itself, with six stops at regular intervals around the lakeshore, which means the fells that ring the lake are very easy to access without the hassle of driving – you can easily reach Walla Crag and Cat Bells for example. The lake is also great for watersports, from a gentle paddle in a canoe to windsurfing – visit Derwent Water Marina at Portinscale for boat rental and instructions.

② Buttermere
MAP C4

Pretty Buttermere is a beautifully sited Lakes village, with high peaks looming above in all directions. It is a haven for walkers, many of whom tackle Haystacks from here; early starts, long hikes and restorative pints at the two excellent pubs here are the order of the day. Otherwise, there is a youth hostel, rooms at the pubs, a campsite with an idyllic setting, and home-made ice cream from Syke Farm Tea Room *(see p101)*.

③ Cockermouth
MAP C2

With its brightly painted Georgian houses and grand Main Street, Cockermouth feels very different from the grey-stone settlements of the national park. The main attraction is Wordsworth House, the birthplace and childhood home of the poet, but simply wandering Main Street, lined with independent shops, is a pleasure in itself. Lose yourself in the town's network of ancient alleyways and courtyards, or enjoy a leisurely meal in one of its many restaurants. In May of odd-numbered years, the town holds a fair to celebrate its Georgian heritage.

Cockermouth's pretty Main Street

4 Mirehouse

MAP D2 ▪ 5 km (3 miles) north of Keswick ▪ 017687 72287 ▪ House open: Apr–Oct 1:30–4:30pm Wed, Sat & Sun; gardens: Apr–Oct 10am–5pm daily ▪ Adm ▪ www.mirehouse.com

The Spedding family,'s stately home, built in the mid-17th century, is one of the most inviting in the Lakes. What distinguishes the house is its serenity and light-filled rooms, and the thought that's gone into making it an attraction for kids with its family nature trail and lovely woodland play areas.

Family friendly Mirehouse

5 Keswick

If you have had a couple of days of walking in the wilds, Keswick will feel downright cosmopolitan – there is a cinema, a theatre, a handful of museums, pubs that fill up at weekends with walkers and locals and a number of decent restaurants and cafés. It does not have the charm of Ambleside or Grasmere, but there is some fine Victorian architecture, and the expansive lakefront, lined with long wooden rowing boats, is very attractive on a summer evening (see pp34–5).

6 Honister Pass

MAP D4

From Buttermere, the narrow road snakes up steep inclines, stark fells rising high on either side, to the final push that takes you to the Honister Slate Mine. This is still a working mine, but it is also a museum and a memorial to the miners who lived and worked and died here in centuries past. Underground tours are

---

OSPREYS IN THE LAKES

In 2001 a pair of ospreys settled at Bassenthwaite, the first time in 150 years that this handsome bird of prey, which feeds exclusively on fish, had been known to nest in the Lake District. Their numbers have since grown considerably, and they can also be spotted at Foulshaw Moss (see p74) and Esthwaite Water (see p28) between April and August.

---

available; the more adventurous can climb the *via ferrata*, or "iron way", on the mountainside. There is also a shop selling slate items (see p99). Beyond the mine, the road slopes down to Borrowdale.

7 Grange-in-Borrowdale

MAP D4

The village of Grange is the gateway to lush Borrowdale, sitting at the valley's northern end. Reached over an old stone bridge, it is an ideal place to rest up after a walk on a summer's day. You can get tea and cake from the teashop, and sit in the garden by the river, watching people amble in over the bridge. This is a low-key but lovely attraction.

Grange-in-Borrowdale's stone bridge

Hikers on the path to Cat Bells

8 Cat Bells
MAP D4

From Hawes End pier on Derwent Water, the path to Cat Bells climbs steeply to 451 m (1,480 ft). The name stems from a Norse belief that the hill was home to a den of wildcats. It is a steep hike, but one that rewards you with a sweeping panorama of the lake on a clear day. On your descent, you could head to the Swinside Inn (see p100), a mile from Hawes End.

9 Castlerigg Stone Circle
MAP E3

Close to Keswick, the Castlerigg Stone Circle is one of the most lovely and theatrical in the country. Comprising 38 stones, it is thought to have been created around 3000 BC. As with all such ancient structures, its exact purpose is something of a mystery, though it may have had an astronomical function.

10 Haystacks

From Buttermere village, many walkers make the iconic 13-km (8-mile) hike to Haystacks, Alfred Wainwright's favourite peak, via Red Pike, High Stile and High Crag. The summit is dotted with tarns, including Innominate Tarn. Wainwright's ashes were scattered here, as he wished, writing: "... if you, dear reader, should get a bit of grit in your boot as you are crossing Haystacks... please treat it with respect. It might be me." (See p24.)

A DRIVE IN THE NORTHWEST LAKES

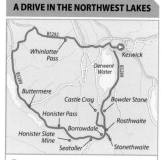

▶ MORNING

From **Keswick**, drive west on the B5292, over the **Whinlatter Pass**. Then take the road heading south and stop at the idyllic village of **Buttermere** (see p95). Take a look at the church of St James, and maybe indulge in a homemade ice cream from **Syke Farm Tea Room** (see p101). From here the road climbs steeply, culminating in **Honister Pass**. At the top you can stop at the **Honister Slate Mine** (see p99), either to buy a slate souvenir, or to take a mine tour. The pass then drops into the greener and more welcoming environment of **Borrowdale**, perfect for gentle exploration. Pass through **Seatoller** (see p98) then divert to **Stonethwaite** (see p98) for a hearty lunch at the **Langstrath Country Inn** (see p100).

AFTERNOON

After having lunch, continue on to **Rosthwaite** (see p98), yet another quaint hamlet with whitewashed buildings. At Rosthwaite you can stretch your legs and burn off a few calories with the footpath walk up to **Castle Crag** (see p98). Further on, make a stop at the National Trust car park for the short walk to the **Bowder Stone** (see p98), an enormous boulder accessed by a wooden ladder. Then cross the river to the idyllic **Grange Bridge Cottage Teashop** (see p101) for a cup of tea and a scone by the river. Drive back to Keswick up the eastern shore of the lake – altogether less hair-raising than the Honister Pass.

See map on p94 ⬅

The Best of the Rest

 Stonethwaite
MAP D4

An ancient settlement, tucked out of the way in the heart of Borrowdale, this small village is home to the renowned Langstrath Country Inn (see p100), named for the looming valley that lies just beyond the village.

 Thornthwaite
MAP D3

An attractive little place with good local walks and an excellent gallery and tearoom, which is a great place to buy local arts and crafts.

 Whinlatter
MAP D3 ■ West of Keswick ■ Visitors' Centre opening times vary, so check website ■ 017687 78469 ■ www.forestry.gov.uk/ whinlatter

This mountainous forest is a great place to go for spectacular views of the Lake District, nature-spotting, mountain biking and walking trails.

Castle Crag
MAP D4

A landmark in Borrowdale, the distinctive Castle Crag is perfect if you fancy a relatively short but satisfying walk. The zig-zag path is steep but not too strenuous.

Bassenthwaite Lake
MAP D2

The highlights of this less-travelled lake include the house and gardens of Mirehouse (see p96) as well as rich birdlife including several magnificent ospreys, which can be observed from viewing platforms (see p96).

Rosthwaite's whitewashed houses

 Rosthwaite
MAP D4

Rosthwaite is a typical Borrowdale hamlet, with whitewashed houses and an excellent local café, the welcoming Flock-In (see p101).

 Caldbeck
MAP E1

This gorgeous village was once home to a number of 17th- and 18th-century mills, but is most famous for the elaborate tomb of legendary local hunter John Peel.

 Seatoller
MAP D4

This is a charming little whitewashed hamlet at the foot of the Honister Pass. It is a great base for walking, with Seatoller House a popular and comfy overnight stop (see p118).

Seathwaite
MAP D4

Sitting at the end of the road, this tiny place gets deluged with visitors as it is the starting point for the hikes to Scafell Pike and Great Gable.

Bowder Stone
MAP D4

One of the region's odder attractions – a gigantic and photogenic boulder brought here from Scotland by a glacier. A ladder helps you to the top.

Bassenthwaite Lake ospreys

Shops and Galleries

 Northern Lights Gallery
MAP T5 ■ 22 St John's Street, Keswick ■ 017687 75402 ■ www.northernlightsgallery.co.uk

A smart commercial gallery that sells original watercolour and oil paintings, prints, drawings, sculpture, jewellery and local pottery and ceramics.

 Castlegate House Gallery
MAP C2 ■ Castlegate House, Cockermouth ■ 01900 822149 ■ www.castlegatehouse.co.uk

This lovely, light- and art-filled house is the best commercial gallery in the Lakes. Exhibitions focus on British art by aspiring and well-known national artists (see p40).

3 **Lakes Distillery**
MAP D2 ■ Setmurthy, near Bassenthwaite Lake ■ 017687 88850 ■ www.lakesdistillery.com

Take a tour of the only distillery in the Lake District, housed inside the stone buildings of a former model farm – and then buy a bottle of their outstanding gin, vodka or whiskey.

4 **Honister Slate Mine Shop**
All sorts of slate items are available at the mine shop, including bird baths, statuary, place mats and made-to-order signs for your house (see p63).

5 **Derwent Pencil Museum Shop**
This place is a treasure trove for budding artists. You can buy absolutely any type or colour of pencil, as well as pastels, sketch pads and all kinds of other artists' materials (see pp34–5).

 Herdy
MAP E3 ■ 8 Tithebarn Street, Keswick ■ 017687 75155

A choice gift shop in the Lake District, Herdy offers homeware and accessories inspired by the delightful Herdwick sheep.

7 **George Fisher Outdoor Shop**
MAP T5 ■ 2 Borrowdale Road, Keswick ■ 017687 72178

Set in a magnificent stone building, George Fisher has everything required for outdoors, with expert help from knowledgeable staff.

Striking exterior of George Fisher

8 **Bitter Beck Pottery**
MAP C2 ■ 11 Market Place, Cockermouth ■ 07803 174120 ■ www.bitterbeck.co.uk

Bitter Beck showcases the ceramics and stoneware of Joan Hardie, whose work is inspired by the natural forms of leaves, bark and lichen.

9 **Thornthwaite Galleries**
MAP D3 ■ Thornthwaite ■ 017687 78248 ■ www.thornthwaitegalleries.co.uk

This respected gallery exhibits and sells the paintings, sculpture, jewellery and pottery of over 100 artists.

10 **Viewpoints Gallery**
MAP T5 ■ St John's Street, Keswick ■ 017687 74449 ■ www.petetasker.co.uk

This gallery features popular local photographer Pete Tasker's pictures of the lakes, tarns and ghylls.

See map on p94

Pubs and Inns

Well-stocked bar of the Dog & Gun

1 Dog & Gun
MAP T5 ▪ 2 Lake Road, Keswick
▪ 017687 73463

The dog-friendly Dog & Gun, in the heart of Keswick, gets packed after Saturday's market. Real ales make it a magnet for walkers year-round.

2 Bitter End
MAP C2 ▪ 15 Kirkgate, Cockermouth ▪ 01900 828993

A traditional English pub, Bitter End serves food, wines and real ales. The Cockermouth Beer Festival is held next door each December.

3 Swinside Inn
MAP D3 ▪ Newlands Valley, Keswick ▪ 017687 78144

A dog-friendly inn, this place provides several options of bars serving good food alongside their own Swinside ales.

4 Kirkstile Inn
MAP C3 ▪ Loweswater
▪ 01900 85219

This 400-year-old inn, between Loweswater and Crummock Water, has open fires and a wealth of history. It serves upmarket dinners and also provides accommodation.

5 Pheasant Inn
It is worth a peek here to feel the atmosphere of an ancient traditional English wayside inn – this place is 500 years old, with log fires and low beams. The 15 en-suite rooms have a lovely country feel *(see p117)*.

6 Bank Tavern
MAP T5 ▪ 47 Main Street, Keswick ▪ 017687 72663

Cask ales and decent pub meals are on offer at this central Keswick pub. There's a beer garden for summer.

7 The Bridge Hotel
MAP C4 ▪ Buttermere
▪ 017687 70252

This fine stone building sits by the bridge in Buttermere; at the Walker's Bar you can have a pint of local real ale and sample Cumbrian pub grub.

8 The Fish Inn
MAP C4 ▪ Buttermere
▪ 017687 70253

This whitewashed hotel in a remote Lakes village was once home to renowned beauty Mary Robinson, known as the Maid of Buttermere – even Wordsworth came to see her.

9 The Wheatsheaf Inn
MAP C3 ▪ Low Lorton
▪ 01900 85199

The 17th-century Wheatsheaf has everything you want in a country pub: a beer garden, an open fire, real ales and pub grub as well as fancier food.

10 Langstrath Country Inn
This family-run inn in the unspoilt village of Stonethwaite started as a miner's cottage in the late-16th century. It is popular with walkers, who welcome the comfort of the cosy, en-suite rooms *(see p119)*.

Restaurants and Cafés

1 The Lingholm Kitchen
MAP D3 ▪ The Lingholm Estate, Portinscale ▪ 017687 71206 ▪ £

Set on the Longholm Estate near Derwent Water, this bright café offers excellent Cumbrian delights.

2 Quince & Medlar
MAP C2 ▪ 13 Castlegate, Cockermouth ▪ 01900 823579 ▪ ££

A lovely wood-panelled dining room where inventive vegetarian food and organic wines are served – it's one of the best in the Northwest.

3 Syke Farm Tea Room
MAP C4 ▪ Buttermere ▪ 017687 70277 ▪ £

At Syke Farm's Tea Room, they serve tasty ice cream home-churned using milk from their own herd of Ayrshire cows. Flavours include Cumberland Ale, Rosehip and Liquorice.

Cottage Teashop at Grange Bridge

4 Grange Bridge Cottage Teashop
MAP D4 ▪ Grange-in-Borrowdale ▪ 017687 77201 ▪ £

A simple but pleasant little place that has a very attractive garden looking out at the river. They serve soup, sandwiches, tea, coffee and cakes.

5 Morrel's
MAP E3 ▪ Lake Road, Keswick ▪ 017687 72666 ▪ £

This comfortable, smart restaurant serves Mediterranean-inspired

PRICE CATEGORIES
For a three-course meal for one with half a bottle of wine (or equivalent meal), taxes and extra charges.

£ under £35   ££ £35–50   £££ over £50

dishes, with a down-to-earth nod towards wholesome British grub. Save space for dessert.

6 Merienda
MAP C2 ▪ 7A Station Street, Cockermouth ▪ 01900 822790 ▪ £

This relaxed and stylish café and bar serves tapas and platters, alongside a range of Fairtrade foods. It prides itself on its excellent coffee.

7 The Square Orange
MAP T5 ▪ 20 St John's Street, Keswick ▪ 017687 73888 ▪ £

This laid-back, continental-style café-bar serves excellent pizzas, tapas and the best coffee in Keswick. There's live music on Wednesday evenings.

8 The Old Sawmill Tearoom
MAP D2 ▪ Mirehouse, Bassenthwaite Lake ▪ £

Opposite the entrance to Mirehouse a simple stone building houses this basic but reliable tearoom. From here, walks radiate in all directions.

9 The Flock-In
MAP D4 ▪ Rosthwaite ▪ 017687 77675 ▪ £

With its punning menu and delightful rustic environs, The Flock-In is a gem of a tearoom. They serve pastries and hearty Herdwick stew with homemade scones.

10 Armathwaite Hall
MAP D2 ▪ Bassenthwaite ▪ 017687 76551 ▪ ££

Experience wonderful fine dining at one of the region's top hotels (see p116). Seasonal, local produce and specialities feature. The hotel also has a more casual brasserie.

See map on p94

TOP10 Whitehaven and Wasdale

Gosforth church

This relatively small area packs in a lot in terms of history and geography, taking you from the once-grand town of Whitehaven, whose buildings reflect the riches harvested during the slave trade, to the increasingly narrow and remote road that runs from the village of Gosforth into majestic Wasdale, a magnet for walkers and adventure-sports enthusiasts. The coast is rather sullied by the major road that runs along it but, in good weather, St Bees is a great place for a swim. Otherwise, go inland for some truly great outdoors.

1 St Bees
MAP A5

There is a substantial stretch of sand beach at St Bees, nicely framed by red sandstone cliffs colonized by sea birds including guillemots, puffins and razorbills. The beach itself is a Site of Special Scientific Interest due to the varieties of crab, mussels and

shellfish that inhabit it. There is also a fine Norman priory here with a wealth of fascinating ancient stone carvings and stained glass to be seen.

2 Egremont
MAP B5

There are two reasons to visit Egremont. One is to see the red

AREA MAP OF WHITEHAVEN AND WASDALE

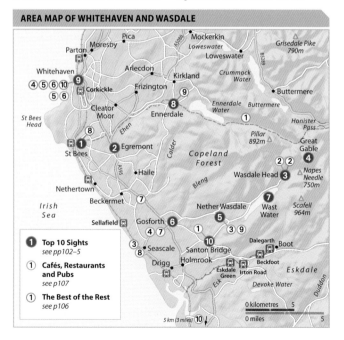

Top 10 Sights
see pp102–5

Cafés, Restaurants and Pubs
see p107

The Best of the Rest
see p106

Egremont's ruined Norman castle

sandstone remains of the Norman castle, built on the site of a Danish fort. The other is the Egremont Crab Fair, which is held in September and has been running since 1267. This has nothing to do with crabs, but refers to the feudal tradition of handing out crab apples to the peasantry. The main events now are the World Gurning (face-pulling) Championships, Cumberland Wrestling and the singing of hunting songs (see p66).

3 Wasdale Head

Fabled for its views and for its role in the development of climbing, Wasdale Head has been on the map for serious hikers for more than a hundred years. The churchyard of tiny St Olaf's (see p33), one of the few buildings at the valley head, shelters the graves of young men who died in early ascents of the peaks here. There is a renowned hotel and pub, a camping shop and a couple of campsites and, of course, the panorama of epic mountains (see pp32–3).

4 Great Gable
MAP D5

Pyramidal Great Gable is easily identifiable from Wasdale Head. If you set your sights on climbing it, then be sure to check the weather first and leave plenty of time for the 900-m (2,950-ft) climb. The beginning of the route, along the valley floor, is interesting – take time to visit the simple little church of St Olaf's, whose beams were made from Viking longships, and note the thick stone walls throughout the valley that were built in the 18th and 19th centuries to pasture sheep.

5 Nether Wasdale
MAP C5

This is one of the prettiest villages in the area, with an open and inviting aspect: a good pub, The Strands Inn (see p107), looks over the manicured village green. The pub provides good accommodation and food and there is a youth hostel nearby, so it is a good base for gentler walks than those on offer at Wasdale Head. You can also access the magnificent valley of Eskdale easily from here.

Stunning scenery at Wasdale and Wasdale Head

Gosforth churchyard

long and with a depth of 79 m (260 ft), it is an impressive sight. At the far end is a National Trust campsite, which makes a good base for exploration. Wordsworth described the lake as "long, narrow, stern and desolate".

 6 Gosforth
MAP B6

This little village is a handy stop for campers on the way to Wasdale, as it has a grocery store and a bakery, as well as a café, restaurant and pubs. The must-see sights are located in the graveyard of St Mary's Church: a tall, slender Viking Cross (see p33) and a cork tree (the most northern in Europe) that was planted in 1833. Inside the church are two "hogback" Viking tombs.

 7 Wast Water
MAP C5

Wast Water sits alongside the road to Wasdale Head, backed by scree-covered slopes: at 5 km (3 miles)

 8 Ennerdale
MAP C4 ▪ www.wildennerdale.co.uk

Ennerdale, the lush and lonely valley to Wasdale's north, is the site of a new development in the Lakes: it has been styled "Wild Ennerdale" by a group that includes the Forestry Commission. The plan is to allow no human intervention, but to observe what occurs in the valley when nature has its way. However, recreation is encouraged: you can cycle or horse-ride along the forest roads, climb Pillar Rock, or walk along Ennerdale Water, fringed by high mountains.

9 Whitehaven
MAP A4

The coastal town of Whitehaven was once the third-largest port in Britain:

Peaceful Wast Water, England's deepest lake

it grew rich on the export of coal and the import of rum and tobacco, as well as on the slave trade. The fine Georgian townscape reflects this former status. While it is evident that the town has fallen on harder times in later years, there have been great efforts to re-energize and develop the harbour for recreation, and it certainly makes an interesting stop-off for a couple of hours.

Whitehaven and its harbour

⑩ Santon Bridge
MAP C6

Santon Bridge, which is located between Wasdale and Eskdale, is another pretty little place, with the Irt flowing through it. You can camp on the lush lawns of the Old Post Office campsite on the banks of the river. The village's main claim to fame, however, is the Santon Bridge Inn, world famous for the long-running Biggest Liar in the World Competition (see p67).

A DRIVE FROM WHITEHAVEN TO WASDALE

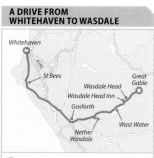

▶ MORNING

Start your day in **Whitehaven**, visiting the harbour and soaking up some of the town's history, either at **The Beacon** or at **The Rum Story** (see p106). The café at The Beacon is a good place for a morning coffee. From here, take the coastal road (which runs parallel to the A595) south, pausing at **St Bees** (see p102) to look at the priory there. Return to the A595, and continue to the village of **Gosforth**, with a stop-off to see the tall Viking Cross in the churchyard. Then head southeast to **Nether Wasdale** (see p103), where **The Strands Inn** (see p107) is an excellent place to stop for lunch.

AFTERNOON

On a clear day, from here the narrow road takes you on the panoramic drive along **Wast Water**, backed by scree that is often reflected in the still water. At the road's end you come to the famously spectacular **Wasdale Head** (see p103), where the valley is perfect for some gentle exploration on foot. You can visit the tiny church of **St Olaf's** (see p106), or simply walk through the valley beside the high stone walls and soak in the mountain views. Dinner is provided at the **Wasdale Head Inn** (see p107), or there is great bar food at the adjoining **Ritson's Bar** (see p58). Hole up either at the inn, or at the basic campsite nearby or the better-equipped National Trust site. Then you are all set to tackle a mountain the following day: Great Gable and Scafell Pike can be accessed from here.

See map on p102 ←

The Best of the Rest

 YHA Black Sail
MAP C4 ■ 0800 0191700 or 01629 592700 ■ www.yha.org.uk
To get away from it all, hike through Ennerdale to the remote YHA (Youth Hostels Association) hostel, a former shepherds' bothy at the top of the valley.

 St Olaf's Church
One of the smallest churches in England, St Olaf's, mostly rebuilt in the 19th century, is one of the few buildings at Wasdale Head (see p33).

3 Seascale
MAP B6
The tiny beach resort of Seascale retains its Victorian charm – even though the Sellafield nuclear power station fills the northern horizon.

4 Crow's Nest, Whitehaven
MAP A4 ■ Whitehaven
A landmark location, in a charming harbour setting, the Crow's Nest is a tall, modern viewing tower. It is spectacularly lit up at night.

5 The Beacon Museum
MAP A4 ■ West Strand, Whitehaven ■ 01946 592302 ■ Open 10am–4:30pm Tue–Sun ■ Adm ■ www.thebeacon-whitehaven.co.uk
This striking building looks like a lighthouse and houses a museum with interactive exhibits.

St Nicholas Church, Whitehaven

6 St Nicholas Church
MAP A4 ■ Whitehaven
The ruins of this old Victorian church have been restored and wreathed with plants and flowers. It forms the centrepiece of a pretty park in the middle of the town.

7 Calder Bridge
MAP B5
Despite being close to the nuclear facility at Sellafield, little Calder Bridge is worth a visit for a stroll to the ruins of a 12th-century abbey.

8 Coast-to-Coast Walk, St Bees
MAP A5 ■ www.coast2coast.co.uk
Devised by Alfred Wainwright, this remarkable long-distance walk takes you from St Bees in the west to Robin's Hood Bay in the east.

9 Ennerdale Bridge
MAP B4
On the route of the Coast-to-Coast walk, Ennerdale Bridge is visited by walkers who cluster in one of the two village pubs. This village is the gateway for visiting Wild Ennerdale.

10 The Rum Story
MAP A4 ■ Lowther Street, Whitehaven ■ 01946 592933 ■ www.rumstory.co.uk
Set in an 18th-century warehouse, this is a good attraction for kids, with plenty of lively tableaux recreating the history of Whitehaven and its connection with the Americas.

The Beacon Museum, Whitehaven

Places to Eat

1 Bridge Inn
MAP C6 ▪ Santon Bridge
▪ 019467 26221 ▪ £

This inn, which hosts the World's Biggest Liar Competition (see p67), is worth a visit at any time for the beer, the food and the warm welcome.

2 Wasdale Head Inn
MAP D5 ▪ Wasdale Head
▪ 019467 26229 ▪ £

The dining room at the inn is oak-panelled, with sepia photos of old climbers on the walls. The food is good, with Herdwick lamb on the menu in season. There are en-suite rooms and apartments (see p119).

Wasdale Head Inn

3 The Strands Inn
MAP C5 ▪ Nether Wasdale
▪ 019467 26237 ▪ £

A handsome village inn with a good reputation for its locally sourced food; they also produce ales and bitters in their microbrewery.

4 The Wild Olive Restaurant
MAP B6 ▪ Gosforth ▪ 019467 25999 ▪ £

This cosy little restaurant, hidden away in Gosforth, is well worth hunting out. Excellent pizzas and pasta dishes, and good for families.

5 Waterfront Restaurant and Bar
MAP A4 ▪ West Strand, Whitehaven
▪ 01946 328184 ▪ ££

Overlooking the marina, this restaurant serves a variety of

PRICE CATEGORIES

For a three-course meal for one with half a bottle of wine (or equivalent meal), taxes and extra charges.
....
£ under £35   ££ £35–50   £££ over £50

dishes. The fish is caught locally from Whitehaven's harbourside.

6 The Wellington Bistro
MAP A4 ▪ The Beacon, Whitehaven ▪ £

At the base of The Beacon Museum and offering nice harbour views, this is a handy daytime stop for substantial and tasty sandwiches and salads.

7 Gosforth Hall Inn
MAP B6 ▪ Gosforth ▪ 019467 25322 ▪ ££

The imposing 17th-century Gosforth Hall is full of quirky architectural detail and is praised for its range of local ales and its pleasant beer garden. The restaurant offers hearty fare.

8 Mawson's Ice Cream Parlour & Coffee Shop
MAP B6 ▪ Drigg Road, Seascale
▪ 019467 29918 ▪ £

Situated near the Seascale beach, this quirky café has a beach hut-themed interior. It serves delicious cakes and ice creams.

9 Low Wood Hall
MAP C5 ▪ Nether Wasdale
▪ 019467 26100 ▪ £

This family-run hotel, set in large gardens and woodland overlooking Nether Wasdale, is one of the few upmarket options in the area.

10 The Byre Café
MAP J3 ▪ Millstones Barn, Bootle, Millom ▪ 01229 718757 ▪ £

Enjoy spectacular views of the Western Fells of the Lake District from the outdoor eating area of this café while savouring traditional Cumberland fare. On colder days, sit by the log burner.

See map on p102

Streetsmart

Sign for a public footpath
at Nest Brow near Keswick

Getting To and Around the Lake District

Arriving by Air

There are no airports in the Lake District. International visitors can fly to **Heathrow**, **Gatwick** and **Stansted** in London, or **Manchester** or **Glasgow** and take trains to Penrith, Oxenholme or Kendal.

Arriving by Train

The **Virgin** West Coast Line between London Euston and Glasgow runs to two main Lake District gateways: Penrith to the north has bus services into the National Park, Oxenholme to the south is 3 km (2 miles) from Kendal and on a branch line to Windermere. Virgin and **First Transpennine** trains run to Oxenholme from Manchester Piccadilly; **Transpennine Express** trains run to Oxenholme, Penrith and Kendal from Glasgow Central.

Book tickets in advance online to get the best deals. **The Trainline** is a useful booking website.

Arriving by Road

The M6 motorway runs through western England between London and the Scottish border, passing to the east of the Lake District. For Kendal, leave the motorway at Junction 36 or Junction 39. For Keswick, leave at Junction 40 (Penrith).

National Express runs long-distance coaches from many British cities to Kendal, Windermere and Penrith.

Getting Around by Local Bus

Stagecoach is the main local bus operator in the Lake District, with buses into the Lake District from nearby towns, including Lancaster, Carlisle, Kendal and Penrith, and linking virtually all main towns during the main Easter–September tourist period. At other times, services can be infrequent or even suspended, and remote corners of the region may not have a bus service at all. Tickets can be bought on board the bus, or a range of passes (including a bus-and-boat combination) are available for 1–7 days of unlimited use.

Getting Around by Local Train

The **Cumbrian Coast Line** between Lancaster and Carlisle serves towns in the western Lake District, including Whitehaven, Grange-over-Sands, Ulverston and Ravenglass (see p53). You will have to change trains along the route, but it is a useful way to reach jumping-off points for the remoter, less-visited western region. Timetables can be downloaded online.

There are two short, narrow-gauge steam train lines within the Lake District. These are of particular interest to rail enthusiasts: the **Ravenglass and Eskdale Railway** (see p53) and the **Lakeside & Haverthwaite Railway** (see p53).

Getting Around by Local Ferries

Cruise boats and ferries operate on several lakes. On Windermere there are both **Windermere Lake Cruises** and the useful **Windermere Vehicle Ferry**, while Coniston Water has the **Coniston Launch** and the **Steam Yacht Gondola**. **Keswick Launch Company** and **Ullswater Steamers** offer cruises on Derwent Water and Ullswater respectively.

Getting Around by Car

While the Lake District's small size should make travelling by car easy, the roads are narrow, winding, often extremely steep and seasonally subject to heavy tourist traffic or to the effects of flooding or snow. Parking is limited in towns and expensive everywhere, even in small villages and remote spots. If possible, leave your car at home, or at least at your accommodation, and make use of buses, bikes, ferries and hiking trails.

However, cars are useful for access to more remote corners of the region, or outside the summer tourist season, when bus services can be limited. Car rental agencies in the region include **Avis**, **Sixt**, **Windermere Car Hire** and **Co-wheels**, which rents out electric cars and twizys. Taxi companies include **Blue Star Taxis** and **Windermere Taxis**, although taking a cab can be fairly expensive.

Getting Around by Bicycle

Cyclists are well catered to in the Lake District, and many places rent out road and mountain bikes. **GoLakes** (see p113), the official website of Cumbria Tourism, has a list of cycle hire stores, and **Mountain Bike Cumbria** is a useful mountain-biking resource. Long-distance routes include the **Cumbria Way Cycle Route** and **Sea to Sea Cycle Route**.

Some local bus services allow bikes on board for a nominal charge, though there are per-bus limits. Cyclist-friendly buses include the 599 between Bowness, Ambleside and Grasmere, and the 525 to Hawkshead, Tarn Hows and Wray Castle.

Getting Around on Foot

The Lake District is criss-crossed with hiking trails, including the 112-km (70-mile) Cumbria Way between Ulverston and Carlisle. The **WalkLakes** and the **Long Distance Walkers' Association** websites have details.

Shorter, tougher hikes include the Old Man of Coniston; Helvellyn via Striding Edge; England's highest mountain, Scafell Pike; or Great Gable. But you'll find far easier strolls too: around lakes, along valleys, or up to scenic viewpoints such as Cat Bells near Keswick.

Always wear top-quality hiking boots and carry water, food and full weatherproof gear. The **Lake District National Park** website (see p113) is a great resource for hiking advice, routes and even guided walks.

DIRECTORY

ARRIVING BY AIR

Gatwick
w gatwickairport.com

Glasgow
w glasgowairport.com

Heathrow
w heathrow.com

Stansted
w stanstedairport.com

Manchester
w manchesterairport.co.uk

ARRIVING BY TRAIN

First Transpennine/ Transpennine Express
w tpexpress.co.uk

The Trainline
w thetrainline.com

Virgin
w virgintrains.co.uk

ARRIVING BY ROAD

National Express
w nationalexpress.com

GETTING AROUND BY LOCAL BUS

Stagecoach
w stagecoachbus.com

GETTING AROUND BY LOCAL TRAIN

Cumbrian Coast Line
w cumbriancoastline.co.uk

Lakeside & Haverthwaite Railway
w lakesiderailway.co.uk

Ravenglass and Eskdale Railway
w ravenglass-railway.co.uk

GETTING AROUND BY LOCAL FERRIES

Coniston Launch
w conistonlaunch.co.uk

Keswick Launch Company
w keswick-launch.co.uk

Steam Yacht Gondola
w nationaltrust.org.uk

Ullswater Steamers
w ullswater-steamers.co.uk

Windermere Lake Cruises
w windermere-lakecruises.co.uk

Windermere Vehicle Ferry
w cumbria.gov.uk

GETTING AROUND BY CAR AND TAXI

Avis
w avis.co.uk

Blue Star Taxis
w bluestartaxis.net

Co-wheels
w co-wheels.org.uk

Sixt
w sixt.co.uk

Windermere Car Hire
w lakeshire.co.uk

Windermere Taxis
w windermere taxisonline.com

GETTING AROUND BY BICYCLE

Cumbria Way Cycle Route
w cumbriaway cycleroute.co.uk

Mountain Bike Cumbria
w mountain-bike-cumbria.co.uk

Sea to Sea Cycle Route
w c2c-guide.co.uk

GETTING AROUND ON FOOT

Long Distance Walkers' Association
w ldwa.org.uk

WalkLakes
w walklakes.co.uk

Practical Information

Passport and Visas

Visitors from the EU, US, Canada, Australia and some other nations do not need a visa to visit the UK. However, you should check entry requirements (which might include proof of funds and a ticket onwards from the UK) on the **UK Government** website. Those who do need visas can apply worldwide at the nearest **UK Visa Application Centre**.

Embassies and High Commissions in London, including those of the **US, Australia, New Zealand** and **Canada** can provide services for their visiting citizens.

Customs and Immigration

Visitors from the EU can bring in unlimited alcohol and tobacco, as long as tax has already been paid and it is for personal use. Arrivals from outside the EU can import 16 litres of beer and 4 litres of wine, along with 1 litre of spirits or 2 litres of fortified wine; 250 g of tobacco; and other dutiable goods of up to £390 in value. Check the website of the UK Government for more detailed information.

Travel Safety Advice

Visitors to the UK can get up-to-date travel safety information from the **US Department of State**, from the **Australian Deparment of Foreign Affairs and Trade** and from the **UK Foreign & Commonwealth Office**.

Travel Insurance

Don't travel without valid insurance and check the policy for how much you can claim for the loss of individual items, and whether you are covered for adventure activities, if relevant.

Health

Britain has no special health issues, but hikers might pick up ticks, which can carry Lyme disease; if you see a tick on your body, contact a doctor or pharmacist promptly. Mosquitoes are rare, but midges (small flies that swarm around still water) are infuriatingly common and can bite, although they don't carry disease. Cover your arms and legs with long-sleeved shirts and trousers, or use a good insect repellent.

All main towns have pharmacies (**Boots** is the most widespread chain); when they are closed, check the window for details of the nearest alternative outlet. UK pharmacists are trained to give advice on basic medical matters. You have to be registered to see an NHS dentist: in an emergency, call the **Dental Helpline** or a hospital.

Britain's **NHS** (National Health Service) provides free emergency treatment, but you will have to pay for specialist care and prescription drugs (unless exempt). Keep receipts for reimbursement.

The following hospitals have emergency departments: **Royal Lancaster Infirmary** (Lancaster), **Furness General Hospital** (Barrow-in-Furness), **Cumberland Infirmary** (Carlisle), the **West Cumberland Hospital** (Whitehaven) and the **Westmorland General Hospital** (Kendal).

Personal Security

Theft and crime is relatively uncommon in the Lake District. Take normal precautions when locking your car and do not leave bags unattended. Report any theft to the police immediately, as you will need a crime report number to make an insurance claim. The local police force in the Lakes is the **Cumbria Constabulary**; you can contact them for any general or non-emergency issues.

Generally speaking, the people you meet, locals and visitors alike, are friendly and open. If you suffer trouble or aggression in any form, report it to the police.

All outlets renting boats, kayaks and canoes should provide a life jacket and a safety briefing. The lakes are cold and deep and can shelve suddenly, so wild swimming is recommended only for competent adult swimmers. Beaches are sand or shingle and gently shelved, but check warning flags for currents.

In an emergency, when contacting the **Police, Ambulance** and **Fire Brigade**, give as precise a location as you can.

Walking and Hiking

The Lake District offers superlative walking and hiking, but rough terrain, variable weather and poor mobile reception mean that you need to be self-reliant and well equipped. Footwear should be tough with a good grip; clothing needs to be warm and weatherpoof; and you should be competent at orienteering in poor visibility. Leave details of your route and schedule with someone reliable who could alert emergency services if you fail to return.

The tide comes in very fast along the Cumbrian Coast, and beach walkers have been cut off and drowned – always check the tide tables on the **BBC** or **Beach Guide** websites before heading out.

Visitor Information

Local tourist offices are in decline, but good websites include the **Lake District National Park, GoLakes, Cumbria Tourism** and **Visit Cumbria**. Locally, your main resource is the **Brockhole Visitor Centre** at Windermere.

The best maps are the Ordnance Survey (OS) range – either the pink Landranger (1:50,000) or the more detailed orange Explorer series (1:25,000). Other options include Harvey's six Lakeland Superwalker water-proof maps (1:25,000). Legendary hillwalker Alfred Wainwright wrote his seven classic *Pictorial Guides to the Lakeland Fells* between 1952 and 1966, and these still provide a unique balance of practical advice and personal guidance for a walk in the region.

DIRECTORY

PASSPORTS AND VISAS

Australia
uk.embassy.gov.au

Canada
unitedkingdom.gc.ca

New Zealand
nzembassy.com/uk

UK Government
gov.uk

UK Visa Application Centre
vfsglobal.co.uk

US
uk.usembassy.gov

TRAVEL SAFETY ADVICE

Australian Department of Foreign Affairs and Trade
dfat.gov.au
smarttraveller.gov.au

UK Foreign & Commonwealth Office
gov.uk/foreign-travel-advice

US Department of State
travel.state.gov

HEALTH

Boots
Branches in Ambleside, Kendal, Keswick, Windermere and elsewhere
boots.com

Cumberland Infirmary
Newtown Road, Carlisle
01228 523444

Dental Helpline
111

Furness General Hospital
Dalton Lane, Barrow-in-Furness
01229 870870

NHS
111 (helpline)
nhs.uk

Royal Lancaster Infirmary
Ashton Road, Lancaster
01524 65944

West Cumberland Hospital
Hensingham, Whitehaven
01946 693181

Westmorland General Hospital
Burton Road, Kendal
01539 732288

PERSONAL SECURITY

Police, Ambulance and Fire Brigade
999 (ask operator for relevant service)

Cumbria Constabulary
101 (non-emergencies)
cumbria.police.co.uk

WALKING AND HIKING

BBC
bbc.co.uk/weather/coast_and_sea/tide_tables

Beach Guide
thebeachguide.co.uk

VISITOR INFORMATION

Brockhole Visitor Centre
015394 46601
brockhole.co.uk

Cumbria Tourism
cumbriatourism.org

GoLakes
golakes.co.uk

Lake District National Park
lakedistrict.gov.uk

Visit Cumbria
visitcumbria.com

Currency and Banking

The British pound (£) is divided into 100 pence (p). Notes are in denominations of £5, £10, £20 and £50; coins are 1p, 2p, 5p, 10p, 20p, 50p, £1 and £2. Banks are the best place for foreign exchange, and are mostly open 9:30am–5:30pm Monday–Friday. Check live currency conversion rates at **XE.com**.

ATMs can be found at banks and supermarkets in all larger towns; some ATMs might charge for withdrawals in addition to whatever charges are levied by your own bank for overseas use. In many villages you can withdraw cash from the Post Office. Credit cards (though often not American Express) are accepted in shops, hotels and bigger restaurants, but you may not be able to use them in B&Bs, pubs and campsites.

Internet and Telephone

Most accommodation, restaurants and cafés in the Lake District have Wi-Fi, usually free for customers. Libraries usually offer free Internet, access for a limited time period. Some tourist offices also have a few terminals for public use.

Phone calls from your hotel room may incur an extortionate mark-up. There are public phone boxes (including some of the traditional red ones) scattered throughout the region; these take credit and debit cards as well as coins, along with prepaid international phone cards (available from post offices and some newsagents).

Use the 5- or 6-digit area code when calling landline numbers within the Lake District. Outside the UK, dial the country code (+44), then the area code without the initial zero.

Mobile coverage of the Lake District is patchy and reception can be poor or non-existent in rural villages or up on the fells.

The UK uses GSM phones with SIM cards. If yours is compatible and unlocked, the cheapest deal is to buy a domestic pay-as-you-go SIM card, which can be topped up at most newsagents. Check with your home service provider about using your phone overseas.

Postal Services

All main towns have a **Post Office**, with local stores often doubling elsewhere. They open Monday–Friday and on Saturday mornings. Stamps are available, singly or in booklets, from newsagents, post offices and large supermarkets.

TV, Radio and Newspapers

There are nearly 500 TV channels available in Britain; what's available will depend on the provider your accommodation has signed up with. **BBC Radio Cumbria** provides updates on local news, weather and sports, as well as interviews on the arts, nature and events.

The region's two main daily papers are the **North West Evening Mail** and the **News and Star**; alongside the weekly **Westmorland Gazette**, **Cumberland &** **Westmorland Herald** and **Cumberland News**. The upmarket **Cumbria Life** is a monthly glossy magazine.

Opening Hours

Shops typically open 9am–5:30pm Monday–Saturday, although hours can be longer in the towns and much shorter in the countryside. Some shops close all of Thursday afternoon.

Time Difference

Britain uses Greenwich Mean Time (GMT) from late October to late March. For the rest of the year it adopts British Summer Time (BST), which is 1 hour ahead of GMT. GMT is 5 hours ahead of US Eastern Standard Time and 1 hour behind Central European Time.

Electrical Appliances

The UK uses three-pin square plugs on 240 volts AC. Most overseas visitors will need adaptors (sold at any electrical store in the UK). North American visitors will probably also need a converter.

Weather

The weather in the Lake District changes rapidly; check the daily forecast online with the **British Meteorological Office** or the local **Weatherline**.

Shopping

The pick of the Lake District's shopping is in the host of available fresh farm- and home-made produce. There's locally bred Herdwick lamb, Cumberland sausages (extremely long, and cooked in a coil), potted shrimps from the coast, cheeses, chutneys and pickles, gingerbread from Grasmere, cask and bottled ales from a dozen or more local breweries, ice cream and seasonal damson gin (made from a local wild plum). You'll also find plenty of studios here selling sculpture, pottery, paintings and photographs (see pp62–3).

Dining

The Lake District is famed for its food, with several Michelin-starred restaurants. In general, the finest dining is in the region's luxury hotels, such as The Samling (see p61), and gastronomes won't want to miss L'Enclume (see p60). Many upper-end places offer a fixed-price lunch, allowing you to enjoy fine dining for a relatively low cost. Some still have a dress code.

Pubs offer very good-value dining in the Lakes, and they are also warm, cosy places to settle down for a pint of ale after a tough day on the fells. Menus tend to revolve around filling meals of the "sausage-and-mash, fish-and-chips, beef-and-ale-pie" variety, although some rise to venison and other seasonal game. A few don't serve food at all.

Cafés are often attached to sights or overlooking famous landscapes, and tend to serve light meals, cakes and afternoon teas. They're often your best bet for vegetarian options. An increasing number of cafés are Fairtrade.

Accommodation

The Lake District's hotels range from secluded, five-star rural estates to handy budget options in the hub towns. Guesthouses and B&Bs may be homely rural getaways or chic boutique options, but all have their own definite character.

You'll find a good choice of well-located hostels, from Windermere lakeside to one remote hilltop option that can only be reached on foot. A few belong to **Independent Hostels UK**, but most are run by the **YHA England & Wales**; members get a cheaper rate, and you can join on the spot. The cheapest beds will be in a shared dorm, but you can also rent twin or family rooms at many hostels. Bunkhouses and barns are another a good budget option; try **Lakeland Camping Barns** or **Find a Bunkhouse**. Prepare for minimal facilities and to provide your own bedding.

Lake District campsites are excellent. Major sites, particularly the **National Trust** campsites, fill up quickly on sunny weekends and during holidays, so it is best to book in advance.

Book accommodation at least a month in advance, especially in peak season (Easter to September) and over Christmas and New Year. Mid-July to September is especially busy, and there is little chance of being able to simply turn up and find vacant accommodation. Peak-season rates are high; at other times there are bargains to be had, especially mid-week.

DIRECTORY

CURRENCY AND BANKING

XE.com
W xe.com

POSTAL SERVICES

Post Office
W postoffice.co.uk

TV, RADIO AND NEWSPAPERS

BBC Radio Cumbria
W bbc.co.uk/radiocumbria

Cumberland & Westmorland Herald
W cwherald.com

Cumberland News
W cumberlandnews.co.uk

Cumbria Life
W cumbrialife.co.uk

News and Star
W newsandstar.co.uk

North West Evening Mail
W nwemail.co.uk

Westmorland Gazette
W thewestmorlandgazette.co.uk

WEATHER

British Meteorological Office
W metoffice.gov.uk

Weatherline
W lakedistrictweatherline.co.uk

ACCOMMODATION

Find a Bunkhouse
W findabunkhouse.com

Independent Hostels UK
W independenthostels.co.uk

Lakeland Camping Barns
W lakelandcampingbarns.co.uk

National Trust
W nationaltrust.org.uk

YHA England & Wales
W yha.org.uk

Places to Stay

PRICE CATEGORIES
For a standard double room per night (with breakfast if included), taxes and extra charges.
£ under £120 ££ £120–£220 £££ over £220

Luxury Hotels

Armathwaite Hall
MAP D2 ■ Bassenthwaite Lake ■ 017687 76551 ■ www.armathwaite-hall.com ■ ££
A stately country house hotel and award-winning spa on Bassenthwaite Lake, Armathwaite Hall is set in 162 ha (400 acres) of deer park and woodland.

Langdale Chase
MAP N2 ■ Windermere ■ 015394 32201 ■ www.langdalechase.co.uk ■ ££
An opulent country hotel, Langdale Chase features a wonderfully atmospheric oak-panelled interior, landscaped gardens, private jetty and an excellent restaurant.

Linthwaite House
MAP N2 ■ Crook Road, Windermere ■ 015394 88600 ■ www.linthwaitehouse.com ■ ££
Among the top Lakes' hotels, Linthwaite House boasts wonderful views of Windermere. The decor is elegant, and the emphasis is on unstuffy comfort and attentive service.

Overwater Hall
MAP D2 ■ Ireby ■ 017687 76566 ■ www.overwaterhall.co.uk ■ ££
This family-owned hotel is a Lakes' favourite, set in a listed 18th-century mansion, which is backed by Skiddaw and surrounded by 7 ha (18 acres) of gardens and woodland. The decor is charming, and dogs are welcome.

Rothay Garden
MAP E5 ■ Broadgate, Grasmere ■ 015394 35334 ■ www.rothaygarden.com ■ ££
This contemporary boutique hotel and spa is housed in a handsome stone building on the edge of Grasmere – Dove Cottage is nearby. There is a lovely lawn dotted with quirky benches, and the food is excellent. Ask for one of the loft suites, which have great views.

Sharrow Bay
MAP G3 ■ Ullswater ■ 01768 486301 ■ www.sharrowbay.co.uk ■ ££
The superb restaurant draws visitors to this comfortable, old-style retreat. Pudding aficionados will be particularly interested in the claim that sticky toffee pudding was invented here.

Gilpin Hotel & Lake House
MAP N2 ■ Crook Road, Windermere ■ 015394 88818 ■ www.thegilpin.co.uk ■ £££
This hotel is run and staffed by people who love their jobs, and this attitude is reflected in the decor, food (see p77) and service. The garden suites are modern and elegant, backed by moors and woodland.

Holbeck Ghyll Country House Hotel
MAP N2 ■ Holbeck Lane, Windermere ■ 015394 32375 ■ www.holbeckghyll.com ■ £££
A handsome country house retreat, Holbeck Ghyll offers Arts and Crafts details and sweeping views of the Langdale Pikes, as well as superb food.

Miller Howe Hotel
MAP N2 ■ Rayrigg Road, Windermere ■ 015394 42536 ■ www.millerhowe.com ■ £££
This Arts and Crafts house has been lovingly restored, with fabulously plush rooms, some with breathtaking views of Windermere. The food is exceptional, so the room-plus-dinner tariff is worth considering.

The Samling
MAP N2 ■ Ambleside Road, Windermere ■ 015394 31922 ■ www.thesamlinghotel.co.uk ■ £££
Perched high above Windermere in a 27-ha (67-acre) estate, the 18th-century whitewashed Samling puts an emphasis on comfort and elegance. The restaurant has a Michelin star (see p61).

Mid-Range Hotels and Inns

Lindeth Fell
MAP N2 ■ Windermere ■ 015394 43286 ■ www.lindethfell.co.uk ■ £
This handsome family-run hotel, overlooking Windermere, is comfortable and has private gardens and a lake. Blackwell (see p15), is a short walk away.

The Brown Horse Inn

MAP N2 ▪ Sunny Bank Road, Winster ▪ 015394 43443 ▪ www.thebrown horseinn.co.uk ▪ ££

This comfy, oak-beamed Winster Valley roadside inn, with 12 en-suite rooms is renowned for its superb restaurant, which uses produce from its own farm (see p61).

Drunken Duck

MAP E6 ▪ Barngates, Ambleside ▪ 015394 36347 ▪ www.drunken duckinn.co.uk ▪ ££

A lovely old inn, Drunken Duck has been stylishly modernized, but retains its exposed beams and open fireplaces. The restaurant (see p60), attracts visitors from all over the world.

The Eltermere Inn

MAP E5 ▪ Elterwater ▪ 015394 37207 ▪ www.eltermere.co.uk ▪ ££

This lakeside country inn is near the pretty village of Elterwater. Guests have access to the nearby Langdale Spa, and the lake is ideal for angling and wild swimming.

Hazelbank

MAP D4 ▪ Borrowdale ▪ 017687 77248 ▪ www.hazelbankhotel.co.uk ▪ ££

A grand Victorian house set in woodland in lovely Borrowdale, Hazelbank has original features including the old servants' bell. The rooms are luxurious, with lovely views.

Lancrigg

MAP E5 ▪ Easedale, Grasmere ▪ 015394 35317 ▪ www.lancrigg.co.uk ▪ ££

This charming hotel specializes in organic, vegetarian cuisine, and in providing a stress-free environment. Massage, Reiki, meditation walks and other therapies are available. The rooms are bright and soothing, some with original plasterwork and lovely views.

Leathes Head Hotel

MAP D4 ▪ Borrowdale Valley, Keswick ▪ 017687 77247 ▪ www.leatheshead.co.uk ▪ ££

Set in the heart of the Borrowdale Valley, this hotel blends Edwardian elegance with modern comforts. The hotel provides various facilities including, free Wi-Fi and a Graphite Bar. Red squirrels can be spotted in the grounds.

Pheasant Inn

MAP D2 ▪ Bassenthwaite Lake, Cockermouth ▪ 017687 76234 ▪ www.the-pheasant.co.uk ▪ ££

This low-beamed, white-washed inn is over 500 years old. Originally a farmhouse, it has been an inn since 1778 and is an atmospheric place to stay.

The Punchbowl Inn

MAP N3 ▪ Crosthwaite, Lyth Valley, near Kendal ▪ 015395 68237 ▪ www.the-punchbowl.co.uk ▪ ££

This venerable Lyth Valley inn has stylish, individually designed rooms, with trendy fabrics, Roberts radios, flatscreen TVs and roll-topped baths. It is also a great option for eating.

Waterhead Hotel

MAP F5 ▪ Ambleside ▪ 08458 504503 ▪ www.englishlakes.co.uk ▪ ££

On Windermere shore, the Waterhead has been converted into a town house-style hotel, with contemporary features.

B&Bs

Ellas Crag

MAP D4 ▪ Stair, Newlands Valley ▪ 017687 78217 ▪ www.ellascrag.co.uk ▪ £

Ellas Crag offers three immaculate rooms in a warm and welcoming guesthouse. Walkers will enjoy the countless valley and fell routes on offer right outside the door.

Fair Rigg

MAP N2 ▪ Ferry View, Bowness-on-Windermere ▪ 015395 48480 ▪ www.fairrigg.co.uk ▪ £

This friendly and efficient B&B occupies a Victorian stone house high above Bowness and looks out to Windermere and the fells around it. Traditionally decorated rooms are spotlessly clean and cosy.

Gilpin Mill

MAP N2 ▪ Crook ▪ 015395 68405 ▪ www.gilpinmill.co.uk ▪ £

A comfortable B&B, Gilpin Mill offers peaceful accommodation with a relaxing south-facing garden. Lake Windermere is just a 10-minute drive away. Bicycles are available to hire.

Kings Arms Hotel

MAP M2 ▪ Market Square, Hawkshead ▪ 01539 436372 ▪ www.kingsarmshawkshead.co.uk ▪ £

This snug old whitewashed pub just off the main square has rooms with exposed oak beams, though the furnishings and bathrooms are modern.

Millbeck Farm
MAP E5 ■ Great Langdale ■ 01539 437364 ■ www.millbeckfarm.co.uk ■ £
Enjoy simple accommodation in a 17th-century farmhouse, with three bedrooms and shared facilities. On the Cumbria Way footpath, it is a popular stop with hikers, who set themselves up for the day with the enormous breakfast.

Sun Inn
MAP M2 ■ Main Street, Hawkshead ■ 01539 436236 ■ www.suninn.co.uk ■ £
This 17th-century village inn has been completely refurbished within, but it retains an antique feel. Rooms are on the small side and patterned with bold wallpaper; one has a huge four-poster bed.

Waterwheel Guesthouse
MAP F5 ■ 3 Bridge Street, Ambleside ■ 015394 33286 ■ www.waterwheelambleside.co.uk ■ £
This little guesthouse is in one of the most picturesque buildings – a 300-year-old cottage looking out to rushing Stock Ghyll and a wooden waterwheel opposite – in a pretty town. Two of the en suites have Victorian clawfoot baths.

Yewfield
MAP M2 ■ Hawkshead Hill, Hawkshead ■ 015394 36765 ■ www.yewfield.co.uk ■ £
This vegetarian B&B in a Victorian-Gothic house is set in 32 ha (80 acres) of land, including wildflower meadows and a coppice garden. It also stages classical music concerts.

The Randy Pike
MAP F6 ■ Low Wray ■ 015394 36088 ■ www.randypike.co.uk ■ ££
This luxurious, Gothic-Revival hunting lodge features imaginative decor and furnishings in three fabulous suites. The locally sourced breakfast is brought to your suite at a time to suit you.

Seatoller House
MAP D4 ■ Seatoller, Borrowdale ■ 017687 77218 ■ www.seatollerhouse.co.uk ■ ££
This 17th-century house with lovely rustic-style rooms preserves the rural peace by having no TV or radio. It is well placed for walks up Great Gable and Scafell Pike, or just a potter around Borrowdale.

Youth Hostels

Elterwater
MAP E5 ■ Elterwater ■ 015394 37245 ■ www.elterwaterhostel.co.uk ■ £
Housed in a gorgeous old farm building, this hostel is a friendly stop for outdoorsy types exploring Langdale. A river rushes by, and the village is one of the most characterful in the Lakes. The Britannia Inn is close by.

Grasmere Independent Hostel
MAP E5 ■ Broadrayne Farm, Grasmere ■ 015394 35055 ■ www.grasmerehostel.co.uk ■ £
Considered the best hostel in the Lakes, this clean, snug place occupies a converted barn on a hillside above Grasmere. There is a great kitchen and a TV lounge with a circular viewing window overlooking the fells.

New Ing Lodge
MAP H4 ■ Main Street, Shap ■ 01931 716719 ■ www.newinglodge.co.uk ■ £
An independent hostel housed in a farm, New Ing Lodge has excellent facilities and two mixed dorms. There is also a small kitchen. It is situated on the Coast-to-Coast walk as well as the Westmoreland Way.

YHA Patterdale
MAP F4 ■ Patterdale ■ 0800 0191700 or 01629 592700 ■ £ ■ www.yha.org.uk
This Ullswater hostel is full of character, with attractive rooms, comfortable beds, open fires and good breakfasts.

YHA Honister Hause
MAP D4 ■ Seatoller ■ 0800 0191700 or 01629 592700 ■ ££ ■ www.yha.org.uk
In an isolated spot on the high Borrowdale to Buttermere pass, this hostel provides breakfast, packed lunches and dinner to hungry hikers.

Hikers Hotels and Camping Barns

The Britannia Inn
MAP E5 ■ Elterwater ■ 015394 37210 ■ www.britanniainn.com ■ £
Sitting on the green in Elterwater, this 500-year-old inn is a good option for walkers who want a little comfort. The rooms have been refurbished in traditional English style.

Brotherswater Inn
MAP F4 ■ Brotherswater, Patterdale ■ 01768 482239 ■ www.sykeside.co.uk ■ £
A family-run venerable old Lakes inn near the

Kirkstone Pass, this place is ideally located for walks in the valley.

Langstrath Country Inn

MAP D4 ▪ Stonethwaite, Borrowdale ▪ 017687 77239 ▪ www.the langstrath.com ▪ £
Converted from a miner's cottage built in 1590, this family-run inn has cosy en-suite rooms and an open fire in the lounge. It also dishes up good local food.

Old Dungeon Ghyll

MAP E5 ▪ Great Langdale ▪ 015394 37272 ▪ www. odg.co.uk ▪ £
In spectacular Langdale at the foot of the fells, the Old Dungeon Ghyll is old-fashioned but comfortable, and has provided a warm haven for walkers for 300 years. The great Hikers' Bar serves real ales and filling food.

Seathwaite Camping Barn

MAP D4 ▪ Seathwaite, Borrowdale ▪ 017687 77394 ▪ £ (£6 per person)
Seathwaite Farm is famed for its wild beauty. There are ten bunk beds and a simple kitchen for self-catering. A remote spot, which is perfect for walks up Scafell Pike and Great Gable.

Swallow Barn

MAP C3 ▪ Waterend Farm, Loweswater ▪ 01946 861465 ▪ www. lakelandcampingbarns. co.uk ▪ £ (£10 per person)
This 17th-century farm barn is in the Loweswater Valley. Electricity, toilets and showers are offered, but bring your own food and sleeping bags with you.

The Traveller's Rest

MAP E5 ▪ N of Grasmere ▪ 01539 435604 ▪ www. lakedistrictinns.co.uk ▪ £
This rugged 16th-century coaching inn is perfect for exploring Grasmere and Dove Cottage, as well as for walking on the fells. The rooms are full of charm and character. The inn's bar also serves a wide range of local ales.

Wasdale Head Inn

MAP D5 ▪ Wasdale Head, near Gosforth ▪ 019467 26229 ▪ www.wasdale. com ▪ £
At the end of a narrow road, this inn boasts the best views in Britain, and has been a haven for walkers since hiking and climbing became popular here. There are ten bedrooms plus self-catering apartments. Good dinners are served, or try Ritson's Bar for pub grub (see p58).

Wythmoor

MAP Q2 ▪ Wythmoor Farm, Lambrigg, Kendal ▪ 01768 774301 ▪ www. independenthostels. co.uk ▪ £ (£10 per person)
This 19th-century barn is less basic than many – showers use solar-heated water and electricity is via a wind turbine.

Campsites

Fisherground

MAP C6 ▪ Fellside Cottage, Eskdale ▪ 019467 23349 or 07580 125952 ▪ www. fishergroundcampsite. co.uk ▪ £ (£7 per person)
Fisherground is absolute heaven for kids – there's a fabulous adventure playground, and it's also a request stop for the steam trains of the Ravenglass and Eskdale Railway

(see p53). Each pitch has its own fire pit.

Gillside

MAP F4 ▪ Gillside Farm, Glenridding ▪ 01768 482346 ▪ www.gillside caravanandcampingsite. co.uk ▪ £ (£10 per person)
On the fellside above Glenridding, this is a friendly farmhouse site with basic facilities. Buy your milk and eggs at the farm and stroll down to the village for shops, pubs and trips on Ullswater.

Low Wray

MAP F6 ▪ Low Wray, near Ambleside ▪ 015394 63862 ▪ www.national trust.org.uk ▪ £
Here you have a choice of wooden pods, camper vans and yurts on the shore of Windermere. You can rent canoes and bikes nearby, and there are leaflets giving hiking and cycling routes.

Sykeside

MAP F4 ▪ Brotherswater, Patterdale ▪ 01768 482239 ▪ www.sykeside.co.uk ▪ £
Magnificent mountain views are the draw at this campsite, with fells such as High Hartsop Dodd providing a great backdrop. There is also a bunkhouse and a bar.

Full Circle

MAP F5 ▪ Rydal Hall, Ambleside ▪ 07811 385870 ▪ www.lake-district-yurts.co.uk ▪ £££ per yurt per stay
Stay for three to seven nights in a traditional yurt that has been adapted for the Cumbrian climate in the grounds of Rydal Hall (see p82). Each yurt has a wood stove, making it snug in winter. Book ahead.

For a key to hotel price categories see p116

General Index

Acknowledgments

Author

Helena Smith is a travel writer and photographer (helenasmith.co.uk). She wrote the *Rough Guide to Walks in London & Southeast England*, and has travelled around the world on photography assignments.

Additional contributor
David Leffman

Publishing Director Georgina Dee

Publisher Vivien Antwi

Design Director Phil Ormerod

Editorial Sophie Adam, Ankita Awasthi Tröger, Rachel Fox, Fay Franklin, Alison McGill, Anuroop Sanwalia, Sally Schafer

Cover Design Richard Czapnik

Design Marisa Renzullo, Bhavika Mathur

Commissioned Photography Helena Smith, James Tye.

Picture Research Subhadepp Biswas, Taiyaba Khatoon, Ellen Root, Rituraj Singh

Cartography Subhashree Bharti, Stuart James, James Macdonald, Reetu Pandey, John Plumer

DTP Jason Little

Production Igrain Roberts

Factchecker Christine Shaw

Proofreader Clare Peel

Indexer Hilary Bird

This book contains OS data © Crown copyright and database rights 2010

Picture Credits

The publisher would like to thank the following for their kind permission to reproduce their photographs:

Key: a-above; b-below/bottom; c-centre; f-far; l-left; r-right; t-top

123RF.com: Duncan Andison 19tl; Kevin Eaves 65cl.

4Corners: Justin Foulkes 48cl; Arcangelo Piai 18-9, 104-5; Sebastian Wasek 11br.

Alamy Stock Photo: A.P.S. (UK) 27cr; Arcaid Images 15cl; britpik 101clb; Adam Burton 2tl, 4cla, 8-9; Sue Burton 53b; Nina Kathryn Claridge 28t; Roger Cope 89b; Cumbriastockphoto 56b; David Tipling Photo Library 98bl; John Davidson Photos 76tr, 106bl; Joe Doylem 58c, 58bl;Kevin Eaves 39tr; economic images 61br; eye35.pix 83tl; Lisa Geoghegan 3tl, 68-9; Louise Heusinkveld 18cla, 98tr; incamerastock 25bl, 52tr; Izel Photography 4cl; James Osmond Photography 32cl; Jason Smalley Photography 16br; Julie Fryer Images 35crb;Joana Kruse 10clb; Keith Larby 99cra; Loop Images Ltd 88cr; David Lyons 12cla; Rod McLean 103b; Anne Elizabeth Mitchell 100t; John Morrison 6br, 16-7, 25tl, 26-7, 27tl, 34-5, 40bl, 44cr, 60br, 65tr; 90b, 93b, 96cl; NDP 70clb; Alan Novelli 4cr, 19cra, 96br; Graham Prentice 84t; PSC-Photography 32bl; Purple Marbles Cumbria 29cl, 59clb; Realimage 97tl; RooM the Agency 4clb; Gordon Shoosmith 62tl; Brian Sloan 105cl; Stewart Smith 32-3; Jon Sparks 29tr, 30cr, 64tl; Stan Pritchard 31cla, 43cla, 102cla; Simon Stapley 31cr; Gary Stones 44bl; travellinglight 10br, 80-1, 95br; Tony Watson 21tl; Mark Waugh 74tl.

AWL Images: Jon Arnold 4b, 86-7; Robert Birkby 1; Paul Harris 33br; Gavin Hellier 35br; Tom Mackie 3tr, 108-9; Travel Pix Collection 11ca, 78cl.

The Dalemain Estate: Dorling Kindersley / Helena Smith 89tr.

Dreamstime.com: Adeliepenguin 11clb; Sue Burton Photography 45t; Davidmartyn 4crb; Chris Dorney 10cl, 20-1, 28br; Drewrawcliffe 30-1, 48-9; Derrick Dunbar 50b; Duncanandison 90tr; Kevin Eaves 7tr, 11tl, 24clb, 42b, 74br; Honourableandbold 51cr; Andrew Howson 7br; Iknowmeinuk 30cla; Eq Roy 14bl; Stocksolutions 33tl; Stunnedmullett 34cl; Victormro 53tr.

Getty Images: Jon Boyes 11cr; Ashley Cooper 21crb; Roger Coulam 46b; DEA Picture Library 38br; Design Pics / Wayne Hutchinson 66c; Julian Elliott Photography 38t, 82b; Cate Gillon 67cla; Heritage Images 40cb; Imagno 17crb; john finney photography 80tl; Nigel Kirby 72cl; Mel Longhurst 71tl; Loop Images / Andrew Stannard 79t; Jeff J Mitchell 39cl; Stock Montage 54cl; Dave Porter Peterborough Uk 13tl, 26clb; Print Collector 55cl; Olaf Protze 12br; Adam Seward 49tl; Brian Sherwen 57crb, 104tl, 106tr; Alan Spedding 77crb; Paul Thompson 47tl; Jill Tindall 51tl; www.mosbornephotography.co.uk 12-3; Andrew Yates 50tl.

Hawkshead Brewery: 76bl; Steven Barber 59tr.

Hawkshead Relish Company: 63cl.

iStockphoto.com: 221A 78bl; Brett Charlton 15bl; ChrisHepburn 94cla; DaveBolton 91cl; DrewRawcliffe 4t; fotoVoyager 64b; golfer2015 95t; JohnPhoenixHutchinson 6cla, 22-3, Jokerbee12 2tr, 36-7; Khrizmo 24-5; mandy_hart 42tc; paulfjs 73cl; George-Standen 72b; Tranquillian1 14c; violinconcertono3 81cl.

Jumble Room: 60cl, 85clb.

Lake District Summer Music Ltd: 66-7.

Lakeland Arts: Blackwell The Arts & Crafts House 45c, 70tl; Abbot Hall Art Gallery 10cr, *The Great Picture* (1646) by Jan Van Belcamp - central panel 41tr; Museum of Lakeland Life & Industry 17tc, 41clb.

The Masons Arms: 58tr.

National Trust Images: Steven Barber 56tl; Andrew Butler 47crb; David Levenson 26br; Nadia Mackenzie 75cr.

Old Laundry Theatre: 67tr.

Old Stamp House: 61cla.

The Quiet Bar: 92cra.

Rex Shutterstock: Ian Rutherford 55tr; Eileen Tweedy 54br.

Robert Harding Picture Library: Ian Egner 20cl; James Emmerson 45br, 103tl.

Sam Read's Bookshop: 13cr.

The Communications Store: L'Enclume 60tc.

Wasdale Head Inn: 107cr.

The Wordsworth Museum and Art Gallery: 10cla.

Yew Tree Barn: 62br.

Cover

Front and spine: **Robert Harding Picture Library:** Jonathan Hodson.

Back: **Dreamstime.com:** Matthew Dixon

Pull Out Map Cover

Robert Harding Picture Library: Jonathan Hodson.

All other images © Dorling Kindersley
For further information see:
www.dkimages.com

Penguin Random House

Printed and bound in China

First American Edition, 2011
Published in the US by
DK Publishing, 345 Hudson Street,
New York, New York 10014

Copyright 2011, 2018 © Dorling Kindersley Limited

A Penguin Random House Company

18 19 20 21 10 9 8 7 6 5 4 3 2 1

**Reprinted with revisions
2013, 2015, 2018**

Published in Great Britain by Dorling Kindersley Limited.

A catalog record for this book is available from the Library of Congress.

ISSN 1479-344X

ISBN 978 1 4654 6779 9

FSC
MIX
Paper from responsible sources
www.fsc.org   FSC™ C018179

SPECIAL EDITIONS OF DK TRAVEL GUIDES

DK Travel Guides can be purchased in bulk quantities at discounted prices for use in promotions or as premiums. We are also able to offer special editions and personalized jackets, corporate imprints, and excerpts from all of our books, tailored specifically to meet your own needs.

To find out more, please contact:

in the US
specialsales@dk.com

in the UK
travelguides@uk.dk.com

in Canada
specialmarkets@dk.com

in Australia
penguincorporatesales@ penguinrandomhouse.com.au

As a guide to abbreviations in visitor information blocks: **Adm** = *admission charge;* **DA** = *disabled access.*